C0-GHR-888

Modern Critical Interpretations

William Shakespeare's Richard II

Modern Critical Interpretations

The Oresteia
Beowulf
The General Prologue to The Canterbury Tales
The Pardoner's Tale
The Knight's Tale
The Divine Comedy
Exodus
Genesis
The Gospels
The Iliad
The Book of Job
Volpone
Doctor Faustus
The Revelation of St. John the Divine
The Song of Songs
Oedipus Rex
The Aeneid
The Duchess of Malfi
Antony and Cleopatra
As You Like It
Coriolanus
Hamlet
Henry IV, Part I
Henry IV, Part II
Henry V
Julius Caesar
King Lear
Macbeth
Measure for Measure
The Merchant of Venice
A Midsummer Night's Dream
Much Ado About Nothing
Othello
Richard II
Richard III
The Sonnets
Taming of the Shrew
The Tempest
Twelfth Night
The Winter's Tale
Emma
Mansfield Park
Pride and Prejudice
The Life of Samuel Johnson
Moll Flanders
Robinson Crusoe
Tom Jones
The Beggar's Opera
Gray's Elegy
Paradise Lost
The Rape of the Lock
Tristram Shandy
Gulliver's Travels
Evelina
The Marriage of Heaven and Hell
Songs of Innocence and Experience
Jane Eyre
Wuthering Heights
Don Juan
The Rime of the Ancient Mariner
Bleak House
David Copperfield
Hard Times
A Tale of Two Cities
Middlemarch
The Mill on the Floss
Jude the Obscure
The Mayor of Casterbridge
The Return of the Native
Tess of the D'Urbervilles
The Odes of Keats
Frankenstein
Vanity Fair
Barchester Towers
The Prelude
The Red Badge of Courage
The Scarlet Letter
The Ambassadors
Daisy Miller, The Turn of the Screw, and Other Tales
The Portrait of a Lady
Billy Budd, Benito Cereno, Bartleby the Scrivener, and Other Tales
Moby-Dick
The Tales of Poe
Walden
Adventures of Huckleberry Finn
The Life of Frederick Douglass
Heart of Darkness
Lord Jim
Nostromo
A Passage to India
Dubliners
A Portrait of the Artist as a Young Man
Ulysses
Kim
The Rainbow
Sons and Lovers
Women in Love
1984
Major Barbara
Man and Superman
Pygmalion
St. Joan
The Playboy of the Western World
The Importance of Being Earnest
Mrs. Dalloway
To the Lighthouse
My Antonia
An American Tragedy
Murder in the Cathedral
The Waste Land
Absalom, Absalom!
Light in August
Sanctuary
The Sound and the Fury
The Great Gatsby
A Farewell to Arms
The Sun Also Rises
Arrowsmith
Lolita
The Iceman Cometh
Long Day's Journey Into Night
The Grapes of Wrath
Miss Lonelyhearts
The Glass Menagerie
A Streetcar Named Desire
Their Eyes Were Watching God
Native Son
Waiting for Godot
Herzog
All My Sons
Death of a Salesman
Gravity's Rainbow
All the King's Men
The Left Hand of Darkness
The Brothers Karamazov
Crime and Punishment
Madame Bovary
The Interpretation of Dreams
The Castle
The Metamorphosis
The Trial
Man's Fate
The Magic Mountain
Montaigne's Essays
Remembrance of Things Past
The Red and the Black
Anna Karenina
War and Peace

These and other titles in preparation

Modern Critical Interpretations

William Shakespeare's

Richard II

Edited and with an introduction by

Harold Bloom
Sterling Professor of the Humanities
Yale University

Chelsea House Publishers ◇ 1988
NEW YORK ◇ NEW HAVEN ◇ PHILADELPHIA

ST. PHILIP'S COLLEGE LIBRARY

© 1988 by Chelsea House Publishers, a division
of Chelsea House Educational Communications, Inc.

Introduction © 1988 by Harold Bloom

All rights reserved. No part of this publication may be reproduced or transmitted in any form or by any means without the written permission of the publisher.

Printed and bound in the United States of America

10 9 8 7 6 5 4 3 2 1

∞ The paper used in this publication meets the minimum requirements of the American National Standard for Permanence of Paper for Printed Library Materials, Z39.48–1984.

Library of Congress Cataloging-in-Publication Data
William Shakespeare's Richard II.
(Modern critical interpretations)
Bibliography: p.
Includes index.
1. Shakespeare, William, 1564–1616. King Richard II.
2. Richard II, King of England, 1367–1400, in fiction, drama, poetry, etc. I. Bloom, Harold. II. Series.
PR2820.W55 1988 822.3'3 87-25674
ISBN 0-87754-936-2 (alk. paper)

Contents

Editor's Note

This book gathers together a representative selection of the best modern critical interpretations of Shakespeare's *The Tragedy of King Richard II*. The critical essays are reprinted here in the chronological order of their original publication. I am grateful to Cornelia Pearsall for her erudite assistance in editing this volume.

My introduction suggests that there is a double Marlovian element in Shakespeare's Richard II; while he subsumes Marlowe's Edward II, there remains a likeness between the rhetoric and psychology of Shakespeare's character and those of Christopher Marlowe himself. Ruth Nevo begins the chronological sequence of criticism with a study of *Richard II*'s genre that develops into an illuminating discussion of what is and is not tragic about Richard.

John of Gaunt's "deathbed eulogy of England" is analyzed by Maynard Mack, Jr., as a study of the nostalgias of kingship. The rhetorical strength of the play's syntax is traced in Gaunt and in Richard by Stephen Booth.

Bolingbroke's usurpation is related by James L. Calderwood to Shakespeare's own sense of "the fall of speech," which the poet-playwright's art must transcend. The opening scenes of *Richard II* are read by Harry Berger, Jr., in a remarkable mode of his own that he calls "psychoanalyzing the Shakespeare text," which is not so much Freudian as it is a shrewd demonstration that current Gallic modes of deconstructing textuality are both anticipated and called into question by Shakespeare's writings.

Something of the Gallic way of reading helps inform Susan Wells's discussion of the theme of subjectivity in *Richard II*. The great Canadian critic Northrop Frye fittingly concludes this volume with a masterly exegesis of Richard II and his play, an exegesis that eschews all textualization, new-fangled and old, in favor of a sense of the wisdom that lies beyond method and theory of language, the wisdom critics once called imagination.

Introduction

There is a general agreement that Shakespeare represents Richard II as a kind of spoiled adolescent (in our terms, not Shakespeare's, since adolescence is a later invention sometimes ascribed to Rousseau). I suspect it might be better to term Shakespeare's Richard II an almost perfect solipsist. He is certainly, as everyone sees, an astonishing poet and a very bad king. The puzzle of the play, to me, is why Richard II is so sympathetic. I do not mean dramatic sympathy, such as we extend to Macbeth, overwhelmed as we are by his intense inwardness. Macbeth is anything but humanly sympathetic. Richard II is, despite his self-pity, his petulance, and a veritable hoard of other bad qualities.

Northrop Frye eloquently calls Richard's "overreacting imagination that sketches the whole course of a future development before anyone else has had time to figure out the present one" a weakness. Pragmatically this is a weakness because it makes Richard doom-eager, but it also renders him curiously attractive, particularly in contrast to the usurper, Bolingbroke. Harold Goddard, whose readings of Shakespeare never leave me, termed Richard "a man of unusual, though perverted, gifts," the principal perversions being sentimentalism and narcissism. Since Shakespeare's most original quality, in my judgment, was the representation of change through a character's self-overhearing, I would call Richard II the first major manifestation of that originality, and I suspect that is why he moves us to a very troubled sympathy. He is indeed a mimesis that compels more of reality to divulge itself than we could have seen without him.

A. D. Nuttall, in his remarkable *A New Mimesis*, the best study of Shakespeare's representation of reality, also emphasizes Richard II's proleptic stance towards his own catastrophe:

> Richard II is plagued not so much by Bolingbroke as by his own capacity for conceptual anticipation: Bolingbroke does not force Richard from the throne, he moves into spaces successively vacated, with elaborately conscious art, by Richard.

A Freudian reading would find Richard an instance of "moral masochism," the collapse of the ego before the superego, sometimes related to strongly manifested bisexuality. But Freud seems to me a codification of Shakespeare, so that a Shakespearean reading of Freud is more enlightening, and shows us that moral masochism is a theatrical tendency in which the ego dramatizes its doom-eagerness in order to achieve a priority in self-destructiveness, so as to anticipate the severity of the shadows of early and abandoned object-affections. Richard II assists at his own crucifixion because he desires a firstness in the exposure of a reality that he knows he cannot master. His perverse, final trace of the royal is to be strong only in his own overthrow.

Since Richard is the anointed king as well as much the most interesting personage in his drama, we are compelled to take his poetry very seriously indeed. There is no one else in Shakespeare's dramas up through 1595 who is anything like his imaginative equal. Had Shakespeare died in 1595, then Richard would have been his principal study in a dramatic consciousness, with Shylock, Falstaff, Rosalind, and Hamlet still to come in the five years subsequent. Until the advent of Hamlet, there is nothing like Richard's eloquence in Shakespearean verse. The edge of that eloquence first troubles us when Richard first despairs:

> No matter where—of comfort no man speak:
> Let's talk of graves, of worms, and epitaphs,
> Make dust our paper, and with rainy eyes
> Write sorrow on the bosom of the earth.
> Let's choose executors and talk of wills;
> And yet not so, for what can we bequeath
> Save our deposed bodies to the ground?
> Our lands, our lives, and all are Bullingbrook's,
> And nothing can we call our own but death,
> And that small model of the barren earth
> Which serves as paste and cover to our bones.
> For God's sake let us sit upon the ground
> And tell sad stories of the death of kings:

How some have been depos'd, some slain in war,
Some haunted by the ghosts they have deposed,
Some poisoned by their wives, some sleeping kill'd,
All murthered—for within the hollow crown
That rounds the mortal temples of a king
Keeps Death his court, and there the antic sits,
Scoffing his state and grinning at his pomp,
Allowing him a breath, a little scene,
To monarchize, be fear'd, and kill with looks,
Infusing him with self and vain conceit,
As if this flesh which walls about our life
Were brass impregnable; and humor'd thus,
Comes at the last and with a little pin
Bores thorough his castle wall, and farewell king!
Cover your heads, and mock not flesh and blood
With solemn reverence, throw away respect,
Tradition, form, and ceremonious duty,
For you have but mistook me all this while.
I live with bread like you, feel want,
Taste grief, need friends: subjected thus,
How can you say to me I am a king?

It is an astonishing outburst, and Richard is crucially changed by it. We may not like him any the better for it, but he is highly conscious of the gap between his royal legitimacy and the luxuriance of his despair. His sense of "the king's two bodies" is more dialectical than that doctrine should allow. Shakespeare's sense of it is very clear; you can celebrate England and its soil if the rightful king is in power, however inadequate he is, but the celebration turns sour if a usurper, however capable, reigns. Richard is both his own victim, or rather the victim of his own imagination, and the sacrifice that becomes inevitable when the distance between the king as he should be and the actual legitimate monarch becomes too great. The shock of his own increasing consciousness of that distance is what changes Richard from a rapacious and blustering weakling into a self-parodying ritual victim. In this change, Richard does not acquire any human dignity, but he does begin to incarnate an extraordinary aesthetic dignity, both lyrical and dramatic. I think he becomes Shakespeare's first implicit experiment in representation, which is to risk identifying poetry and a national ritual sacrifice. The risk is not that Richard will fail to be persua-

ST. PHILIP'S COLLEGE LIBRARY

sive, but that he will put poetry and its powers of representation into question.

His rhetoric of pleasurable despair is more than oxymoronic, and enforces the lesson that Nietzsche learned from the poets; what makes representation memorable is pleasurable pain, rather than painful pleasure. I know of many readers and students who agree with Dr. Samuel Johnson in his judgment that *Richard II* "is not finished at last with the happy force of some other of his tragedies, nor can be said much to affect the passions, or enlarge the understanding." Yet even these recalcitrants thrill to the justly famous cadences of: "For God's sake let us sit upon the ground / And tell sad stories of the death of kings." I think of Hart Crane's marvelous variation upon this in *Voyages* VI:

> Waiting, afire, what name, unspoke,
> I cannot claim: let thy waves rear
> More savage than the death of kings,
> Some splintered garland for the seer.

Crane shrewdly interprets Shakespeare as associating the death of kings and the splintering of poetic wreaths. Dr. Johnson, best of critics, was too unmoved by *Richard II* to achieve an accurate sense of the king's transformation:

> It seems to be the design of the poet to raise Richard to esteem in his fall, and consequently to interest the reader in his favour. He gives him only passive fortitude, the virtue of a confessor rather than of a king. In his prosperity we saw him imperious and oppressive, but in his distress he is wise, patient, and pious.

In his fall, Richard is not wise but eloquent, not patient but driving towards death, not pious but a kind of Christ-parody. His wounded narcissism is augmented by the turning of his aggressivity against himself, and he overgoes Marlowe's Edward II as a rhetorician of self-pity:

> They shall be satisfied. I'll read enough,
> When I do see the very book indeed
> Where all my sins are writ, and that's myself.
> Give me that glass, and therein will I read.
> No deeper wrinkles yet? Hath sorrow struck
> So many blows upon this face of mine,

And made no deeper wounds? O flatt'ring glass,
Like to my followers in prosperity,
Thou dost beguile me! Was this face the face
That every day under his household roof
Did keep ten thousand men? Was this the face
That like the sun, did make beholders wink?
Is this the face which fac'd so many follies,
That was at last out-fac'd by Bullingbrook?
A brittle glory shineth in this face,
As brittle as the glory is the face,
[*Dashes the glass against the ground.*]
For there it is, crack'd in an hundred shivers.
Mark, silent king, the moral of this sport,
How soon my sorrow hath destroy'd my face.

The outrageous parody of Marlowe's Faustus celebrating Helen is scarcely an accident in a play that subsumes Marlowe's *Edward II.* By associating Richard with two of Marlowe's antiheroes, Shakespeare suggests a likeness between his Richard and the self-destructive, narcissistic great poet who was Shakespeare's closest precursor. It may seem fantastic to suggest that the aura of Christopher Marlowe seeps into the rhetoric and psychology of Richard II, but this was a complex trick that Shakespeare was to play again. The fine symbolic gesture of dashing the mirror to pieces is wholly appropriate for the Marlovian protagonists, and for Christopher Marlowe's own fate. Here as elsewhere Shakespeare is warning himself (and us) that Marlowe's way was not to be taken up.

Formally, *Richard II* is a tragedy, as Johnson took it to be, but it is the tragedy of a self-indulgent poet rather than the fall of a great king. The dashing of the glass is also the destruction of the legitimate royal countenance, yet when Richard is murdered we do not experience the shock of a monarch dying. Hamlet, who never ascends a throne, dies more than royally, but Richard's apparent courage when he kills the attendants is precisely what Goddard called it: "the reflex action of a man without self-control in the presence of death." There is aesthetic dignity in Richard's rhetoric of decline and fall, but not in the actual way that he dies. It is the death of the poet who has not matured into the possession and representation of wisdom.

The Genre of *Richard II*

Ruth Nevo

Beyond the woeful or happy outcome brought about by the catastrophe Elizabethan dramatic theory did not distinguish between the structure of tragedy and comedy; neither were the dramatic practitioners possessed of a theory of genre which would enable them to distinguish with any rigor between tragedy and history. Polonius's familiar puzzlement is not only his own but the age's failure to achieve radical definitions. Thus the "chronicle" plays of the period, which deal with the fall of princes, great changes of fortune, tyrannical intrigues, and Machiavellian betrayals, based upon no clear generic principle of either tragedy or history, based, indeed, at best upon a *de casibus* interpretation of events indifferent to the distinction, present a bewildering medley of hybrids, a spectrum of mixed or intermediate tints. And whether any given instance is an example of "tragicall historie" or historical tragedy or of English Seneca requires a more systematic philosopher than Polonius to determine. Both *Richard III* and *Richard II,* though integral parts of their respective historical tetralogies, are called "tragedies" in the Folio and in the Quartos upon which it was based.

Shakespeare, therefore, found few clear conceptions of genre ready to hand. Nor did he possess a theory of tragic character. He invented as he went along; and as he proceeds from the histories to the tragedies, his exploratory, creative deployment of his art discovers and establishes the distinctions that he needs. The chief distinction between

---

From *Tragic Form in Shakespeare.* © 1972 by Princeton University Press.

history and tragedy rests in the restructuring the narrative undergoes in order to bring out the protagonist's personal responsibility for events and his personal response to them. It is his distinctive aspiration, will, or purpose that becomes salient. In the history plays the protagonists are exhibited as struggling for freedom to initiate events. Even that artist in villainy, Richard III, has not fully escaped from the destined role of a scourge of God. If they are made vivid, it is by a degree of idiosyncrasy in their response to their destined roles, but they are nevertheless governed by an overall ironic process of history. If we may imagine them as figures in bas-relief compared to the sculptures in the round of the tragedies, they may also thus be compared with the tapestry figures of pure chronicle. But in *Richard II* the providentialist view of events which dominated Shakespeare's historical sources gives way to a rival concern. In *Richard II* Shakespeare's tragic idea takes the form of a development in the dimension of character that is decisive for future directions.

The play's overt conflict is between the strong and successful Bolingbroke and the vain and vacillating Richard; and looked at from the point of view of the management of events, the play is well made, Richard's decline and Bolingbroke's rise crisscrossing effectively in the center. But the simple fall-rise pattern does not exhaust the potentialities of the dramatic material as Shakespeare presents it. The play is not contained without remainder, so to speak, within the historical pattern. The remainder inheres in the characterization of Richard, in which the play's distinction lies. It is this study of the complex figure of the tragic hero that exerts pressure upon the shape of the play, so that from within the episodic chronicle form we perceive the emergence of what we can recognize, in the light of our knowledge of the later tragedies proper, as the distinctively tragic structure. The play does not exhibit the consummate articulation of phases of the great tragedies. The first two acts are episodic and the study of tragic character does not really get under way until the peripeteia of act 3. And when it does it is almost, though not quite, independent of the content of acts 1 and 2. But the play does possess a movement which approximates to that of the great tragedies. Coleridge's remark concerning Richard's "continually increasing energy of thought, and as constantly diminishing power of action" takes on an added significance when to Coleridge's psychological interest in character portrayal is added an interest in the structure of tragedy that directs us to search for the principle informing this movement.

As act 1 proceeds we perceive, through the considered juxtaposition of scenes, the predicament in which Richard is placed. The act is composed primarily of two scenes of elaborate formal challenge between rival claimants for justice. At three points, however, the façade of highly ceremonial assertion and counterassertion between Bolingbroke and Mowbray is rent to provide a glimpse of the historical actualities that lie behind these rituals. The inserted dialogue (1.2) between Gaunt and the Duchess of Gloucester points to the hidden and ambiguous source of all the trouble: the murder of Woodstock; the final scene of the act indicates, possibly, the real import both of Richard's fear of Bolingbroke (his courtship of the common people) and of Bolingbroke's challenge of Richard. (Though Holinshed, and Bolingbroke himself, in *2 Henry IV* [3.1.72–74] deny the imputation of forethought: "Though then, Heaven knows, I had no such intent, / But that necessity so bow'd the state, / That I and greatness were compell'd to kiss.") And the dialogue between Richard and Gaunt after the sentence of banishment makes clear the nature of the political arrangement that has taken place behind the scenes to make the present solution feasible. To Gaunt's lament for his son's exile Richard replies:

> Thy son is banish'd upon good advice,
> Whereto thy tongue a party-verdict gave:
> Why at our justice seem'st thou then to lour?
>
> (1.3.233–35)

And Gaunt's reply admits his complicity:

> Things sweet to taste prove in digestion sour.
> You urg'd me as a judge, but I had rather
> You would have bid me argue like a father.
> O, had it been a stranger, not my child,
> To smooth his fault I should have been more mild.
> A partial slander sought I to avoid,
> And in the sentence my own life destroy'd.
> Alas, I look'd when some of you should say
> I was too strict to make mine own away;
> But you gave leave to my unwilling tongue
> Against my will to do myself this wrong.
>
> (1.3.236–46)

What is presented then is the tangential relationship between the dramatized conflict of wills and the complex reality of history, where political morality or amorality is still further complicated by the blood relationship between the various contenders for power. Feudal rituals mask the ulterior political realities of collusion and guilt. In the predicament thus presented, power and justice are divided and disjoined. And it is in these circumstances that the King must play his allotted role. Richard must rule, in his circumstances, either by what the Elizabethans, following Machiavelli, called *virtù,* or by that older dial of princes called virtue. He must govern by either power or justice, since the breach between them already exists.

When we ask what is wrong with Richard's interruption of the lists, an act for which he has been richly and variously scolded by his severer critics, we are forced to the conclusion that it represents no more, but also no less, than simple political expediency, in circumstances which leave little other alternative. Later in the play we are given a parallel scene in which we watch Bolingbroke, at the height of his power and success, encountering a similar situation. And the comparison is instructive.

Once again the question at issue is Gloucester's death. Bagot is now the chief witness and Aumerle the accused, as Mowbray was accused by Bolingbroke in act 1. Once again the situation shapes itself in terms of the challenges and counterchallenges of honor, with the civil dissension inherent in the situation made manifest by the successive involvement on one side or the other of Fitzwater, Surrey, and Percy. The question, by an evident irony, circles back to the original contender, Mowbray, and we are only prevented from finding ourselves, so to speak, back at base, by Mowbray's death meanwhile in exile. But what is significant is that Bolingbroke, too, can do no more than shelve the whole matter, leaving the contenders under gage, "Till we assign you to your days of trial." The intransigeance of the original ugly fact is a perpetual stumbling block to the house of Edward's sons, those "seven vials of his sacred blood" which has been shed. Thus the ultimate source of evil in this play and those which follow it (in the chronology of history, not by date of composition) is clearly identifiable. It is Woodstock's murder—a crime which sets up the chain reaction of violence and counterviolence, of guilt and the incurring of guilt, that scourges England through half-a-dozen reigns. But if Woodstock's death is the ultimate cause of these events, it is nevertheless not what is dramatized in *Richard II.* The play leaves this original act of Cain in impenetrable obscurity; but it presents Richard, at the outset, in precarious command of a dangerous and complex situation. He cannot place his dubious position at hazard upon the outcome of the duel, and he certainly cannot circumvent the challengers without the behind-the-scenes political arrangements we observe. This is Richard's predicament; and what the first two acts are engaged to exhibit is his disastrous incapacity to establish his ascendancy.

Richard's handling of the difficult situation presented in act 1 is, I have suggested, not unmarked by a shrewd political acumen. But it is marred by levity. His speech to the combatants, in the high vein of prophetic patriotism which is struck again and again, and with the utmost seriousness, throughout the play, has impressive dignity:

> For that our kingdom's earth should not be soil'd
> With that dear blood which it hath fostered;
> And for our eyes do hate the dire aspect
> Of civil wounds plough'd up with neighbours' sword,
> And for we think the eagle-winged pride
> Of sky-aspiring and ambitious thoughts,
> With rival-hating envy, set on you
> To wake our peace, which in our country's cradle
> Draws the sweet infant breath of gentle sleep.
>
> (1.3.125–33)

But behind the regal bearing and the regal gesture is revealed Richard's dismal lack of that inalienable personal power which a later age would come to call charisma, and which alone could carry him through. He has not that in his face which either Mowbray or Bolingbroke would feign call master. And this is made manifest by their refusal, insolent in Bolingbroke's case, conciliatory in Mowbray's, to obey him, notwithstanding the brave show of "lions make leopards tame" or "we were not born to sue, but to command." The dramatic conduct of the first scenes throws into relief the "high pitch of the contender's resolution," rather than any high pitch of the King's. And though divinity hedges him (Gaunt will raise no hand against the Lord's anointed despite the appeal of his widowed sister-in-law) we are left with the overriding impression of a precariousness in his exercise of authority. The main source of this impression lies in the frivolity of Richard's attitude to Gaunt. The first note of this frivolity is heard in the flippant "pluck'd four away" with which Richard announces his commutation of Bolingbroke's sentence, and the scarcely veiled effrontery of "Why, uncle, thou hast many years to live." It is the note, or the major chord, upon which act 1 closes:

Now put it, God, in the physician's mind
To help him to his grave immediately!
The lining of his coffers shall make coats
To deck our soldiers for these Irish wars.
Come, gentlemen, let's all go visit him,
Pray God we may make haste and come too late!
(1.4.59–64)

This is the mainspring of the development in act 2. For if in act 1 was revealed Richard's lack of *virtù*—he plays neither lion nor fox with sufficient conviction—in act 2, against the powerful remonstrance of the dying Gaunt, is revealed his lack of virtue. And much is to be learned from the way in which this lack of virtue is in fact revealed. As we have seen, act 2 is the phase of tragedy which presents the tempting or testing of the protagonist in terms of personal decisions which have to be made. Richard's "Can sick men play so nicely with their names?" and "A lunatic lean-witted fool, presuming on an ague's privilege," contrasting with the passion of Gaunt's "Landlord of England art thou now, not king," represent not merely a callous indifference to mortal illness, but a deliberate refusal to entertain the seriousness of the issues. Thus it is Richard's flippancy, exhibited in the deathbed confrontation with Gaunt, that indicates the nature of his "temptation." The difficulty is that the king's frivolity is exhibited only in the passage with Gaunt and made only by implication to bear the whole brunt of the indictment against him. It is by narrative hearsay that we are informed of Richard's unstaid youth, light vanity, the thousand flatterers which sit within his crown, the throne's bankruptcy, the shame of the leasing out of English land, and the burdensome exactions and taxes under which groan commons and nobles alike—charges which are made to account for the defection of Willoughby, Ross, and Worcester. But these defects and abuses are given no self-reflection or reverberation or internalization in Richard's mind, nor are they mediated by some powerful private motivation with which he must engage. Marlowe did better with his Edward in this respect.

Whether this summary fashion is due, as Rossiter thought, to Shakespeare's leaning too heavily (by allusion) upon *Woodstock* is less to the purpose than the perception that in the encounter between uncle and nephew is encapsulated the morality content of the older play. There Richard's three uncles exhort him to virtue, and Tresilian, Bushy, and Green to vice; the familiar form of the medieval debate constitutes the whole structural frame of *Woodstock*. It is noteworthy that in *Richard II* this psychomachia is reduced to one stage of a process, in keeping with the new kind of structure and the new kind of tragic issue toward which Shakespeare is evidently feeling his way. But the treatment suffers from too radical an abridgement. The effect is of a dramatic thinness, or flatness, or absence of relatedness. The discontinuity, the gaps, so to speak, between given, fixed aspects or attributes of character (regality, levity) are not only too great but also too empty of reflection to allow that play of inference which alone constitutes psychological density and creates our sense of character. Shakespeare overcomes this dramatic thinness in an impressively skillful manner through his presentation of the role of York. But this is still in the earlier episodic mode, not capable of the effects of integration later achieved.

York, upon Bolingbroke's return, becomes a vessel of ambivalence, swaying between fealty and justice, dynastic legitimacy and virtue. This is the conflict which Richard's frivolity imposes upon his subjects; it is also a continuation of the conflict implicit in the play's predicament. For as Bolingbroke presents his case to York it becomes abundantly clear that whichever principle York chooses he must do violence to another no less imperative.

> Will you permit that I shall stand condemn'd
> A wandering vagabond, my rights and royalties
> Pluck'd from my arms perforce, and given away
> To upstart unthrifts? Wherefore was I born?
> If that my cousin king be King in England,
> It must be granted I am Duke of Lancaster.
> You have a son, Aumerle, my noble cousin;
> Had you first died, and he been thus trod down,
> He should have found his uncle Gaunt a father,
> To rouse his wrongs and chase them to the bay.
> (2.3.118–27)

The dichotomization of values is complete, and York mirrors the conflict which is externalized, in the plot, in the struggle between the two contenders for the crown. But he does not mirror a dilemma within the soul of the protagonist, as, for instance, does Enobarbus; he merely substitutes for it. Maynard Mack has spoken of "umbrella" speeches or episodes, those mirrors of analogy in the mature Shakespearean drama "under which more than one consciousness shelters."

These are screens, he says, citing Lear's Fool, Poor Tom, Enobarbus, and the sleepwalking Lady Macbeth, on which "Shakespeare flashes, as it were, readings from the psychic life of the protagonist." York is incipiently such a figure, but it is not until the end of the play, as I shall presently show, that the readings flashed onto the screen he provides are from the psychic life of Richard himself.

In act 2 we watch the actualization of Gaunt's prophecy: the callous indifference of Richard to his death, the seizing of Bolingbroke's inheritance, the defection of Willoughby, Ross, and Worcester, and the mournful forebodings of the Queen. It is the expropriation of Bolingbroke, of course, that makes possible his return as claimant for simple justice. But the fatality of this act, which in fact precipitates Richard's downfall, is obscured by the secondary issues, so that its effect is dissipated in a catalogue of political abuses of which the expropriation of Bolingbroke appears to be only one. We are thus catapulted straight into the peripeteia of act 3—the unkinging of the King—with no transition other than the episodic reference to the Irish expedition by Bushy, Green, and Bagot. These scapegoat figures, caterpillars of the commonwealth, serve the ends of historical apologetic for the sweet English rose, but they usurp attention that should be concentrated upon the figure of the tragic hero. What Shakespeare, it seems, has not mastered in this play is the foregrounding of the fatal choice—the act, portentous in the inescapability of its consequences, fully expressive of the protagonist's nature (though it may be unpremeditated) which precipitates both disaster and the recognitions that constitute the emergence of tragic consciousness in one who is, paradoxically, both agent and victim of his fate.

Because Shakespeare has thus failed to bring out and make salient the tragic error, act 3 appears to set off, so far as the character of Richard is concerned, in a completely new direction. The effect of discontinuity, of too sudden a shift of focus, is the result of an insufficient anchoring of present responses in purposes, feelings, desires, intentions previously entertained. By the time Shakespeare comes to write *Lear,* in which so much that is implicit in *Richard II* is developed, and *Macbeth,* in which so much that is implicit in *Richard III* is developed, he will know how to exploit a tragic error committed at the outset of the events. Richard's tragic life begins, in effect, only in act 3 itself; unlike Lear and Macbeth, he is not yet possessed of that great tragic asset, a past—is not yet haunted and hounded by the memory of that which is done. It is precisely, indeed, toward a realization of the nature of his temporal existence that he is made to struggle in act 3. And it is this which gives one the sense of being in the very forge and workshop of Shakespeare's art. For it is the "inside of the event" that we are given throughout these central perturbations in act 3, the very process of Richard's discovery of self. Those critics who complain of "self-dramatization" overlook the fact that for a character to have a self to dramatize is one of the more remarkable achievements of European literature. The question is important enough to warrant a moment's digression.

In *Richard III* Shakespeare had achieved a density of characterization by the essentially simple device of impersonation, which was his inheritance from the Devil-vice figure of the moralities. Richard not only acts the villain; he delights in the exercise of his skill as an enactor of villainy. He is both actor and *régisseur* of his own part, and the fascination of the performance hinges upon the very ambiguity of the notion of playacting, interchangeably illusion and reality. All reference in Shakespeare to playacting, direct or implicit, has this effect, creating a metatheatre in which levels of representation interact. The same principle accounts for the density of Falstaff. And in the multiplication of possibilities of interplay between the projection, the performance, the assessment, and the awareness of a role lies the inimitable impression of exuberance and zest which mark both characters, each in his own mode. The moment, however, we are tempted or invited to probe behind a public role to a private reality, to press beyond the imitation of a histrionic toward the imitation of an historic mode of existence, we find that such characters become dynamic in a totally new way. A principle of growth, of modification, of real human development is introduced into figures which, whatever their versatility, are tied to the irreducible fixity of Crookback or Fatbelly. Falstaff as comic character cannot truly survive the sense of self which is beyond the sense of role. Hence the notorious fracture, so to speak, of the whole conception, in *2 Henry IV*. In Richard, on the other hand (since by a paradox of terminology, it is the tragedies which explore the "historic," or inward, as opposed to the "histrionic," or outward, mode of existence), we perceive, in his soliloquy after the dream, the very point of emergence of a new possibility: a dialogue of self and soul.

> Give me another horse, bind up my wounds:
> Have mercy Jesu! Soft, I did but dream.

O coward conscience! how dost thou afflict me?
The lights burn blue. It is now dead midnight.
Cold fearful drops stand on my trembling flesh.
What do I fear? myself? There's none else by,
Richard loves Richard; that is, I am I.
Is there a murderer here? No; yes, I am:
Then fly. What from myself? Great reason why?
Lest I revenge. What, myself upon myself?
Alack, I love myself. Wherefore? For any good
That I myself have done unto myself?
O no! Alas, I rather hate myself
For hateful deeds committed by myself.
I am a villain: yet I lie, I am not.
Fool, of thyself speak well: fool, do not flatter.
My conscience hath a thousand several tongues,
And every tongue brings in a several tale,
And every tale condemns me for a villain;
Perjury, in the high'st degree,
Murder, stern murder, in the dir'st degree;
All several sins, all us'd in each degree,
Throng to the bar, crying all, Guilty! Guilty!
I shall despair. There is no creature loves me;
And if I die no soul shall pity me.
Nay, wherefore should they? Since that I myself,
Find in myself no pity to myself?

(*Richard III,* 5.3.178–204)

It is rudimentary, though powerful; it is the merest sketch—too little and too late. But it is of the highest significance. And it is the germ which will develop through subsequent plays, adding to dramatic character an entire inner dimension of tragic self-discovery.

It is thus not further evidence of Richard's failure as a king that we are invited to perceive throughout act 3. His failure as a king has been sufficiently established, as has Bolingbroke's cool confidence and masterly practicality. We are invited to perceive, stage by stage, through the direct disclosure of monologue and through inferences that the detail of the language enables us to make, a total curve of experience. The emotions that constitute that experience—shattered confidence, the sense of inadequacy, impotence, humiliation, grief—find cumulative expression throughout Richard's speeches in acts 3 and 4 and culminating expression in the speech at Pomfret. And their delineation of emerging self-awareness and the struggle for self-possession is masterly. We have been misdirected to find in these speeches the luxuriatings in misery of a "poet *manqué*, who loved words more dearly than his Kingdom," or a dilettante sentimentalist, "morbid, vacillating, impotently reflective and emotional," "whose tragedy expresses itself in terms that clearly point to the weakness [acute self-consciousness] that has been, in part, its cause." These speeches are properly to be construed not as educing the cause of his fall before the onslaught of Bolingbroke, but as the consequences of that fall, suffered, known, experienced, and reflected in the mind. Self-dramatization (Eliot's notorious stricture upon Othello) is the very medium of the art of tragedy, the method whereby it articulates its progress. It is as fallacious to regard it as an idiosyncrasy which demands particularistic psychological explanation as to construe the sculptured immobility of the discus-thrower as an indication of his curious inability to throw a discus. How shall we become aware of a character's thoughts save by his utterance of them, of a character's emotions save by his expression of them, of a character's possession of self save by his manifestation of a consciousness of self, or of a character's tragic identity save by his tragic agon, his pressing to the limit the experience of adversity in existence. The tragic hero is locked in struggle with himself, like Jacob with the angel.

As Moulton perceived, this fall of Richard is constructed on Shakespeare's favorite plan: "its force is measured, not by suddenness or violence, but by protraction and the perception of distinct stages" (*Shakespeare as Dramatic Artist*). Aristotle's anagnorisis—the transformation of ignorance into knowledge through recognition of identity—provides the paradigm for all such transmutations in tragedy. What distinguishes the Shakespearean kind is the richness, depth, inwardness, and range of awareness which the expressive, self-revelatory, self-exploratory speech of the hero enables him to articulate. In Greek drama what is recognized is identity. In Shakespearean drama what is recognized is self. Characteristically the self-exploration is given substance and definition by the terms of the psychomachia set forth in act 2. And though this, as we have seen, is less than sufficiently "done" in this play, nevertheless particular analysis of the self-exploration of Richard shows that the observation holds good here too.

Richard's vacillations are a function basically of that failure to summon up the maximum resources of the will, that lack of self-confidence, which characterizes men who are weaker than the opponents they encounter. But the substance of his vacillations consists of desperate recurrent attempts to achieve or fix an image of himself with which he can live should his native role slip from his grasp.

When we first encounter Richard upon his return from Ireland, weeping for joy to stand upon his kingdom once again, the speech is in direct emotional continuation of his address to the combatants in act 1, in which he adjured them to protect the peace "which in our country's cradle / Draws the sweet infant breath of gentle sleep" (1.3.132).

> Dear earth, I do salute thee with my hand
> Though rebels wound thee with their horses' hoofs.
> As a long-parted mother with her child
> Plays fondly with her tears and smiles in meeting,
> So weeping, smiling, greet I thee, my earth,
> And do thee favours with my royal hands;
> Feed not thy sovereign's foe, my gentle earth,
> Nor with thy sweets comfort his ravenous sense,
> But let thy spiders that suck up thy venom
> And heavy-gaited toads lie in their way,
> Doing annoyance to the treacherous feet,
> Which with usurping steps do trample thee.
>
> (3.2.6–17)

These speeches are in marked contrast with the historically oriented nationalism of Gaunt's prophecy:

> This royal throne of kings, this scept'red isle
> . . . .
> This happy breed of men, this little world
> . . . .
> This blessed plot, this earth, this realm, this England,
> This nurse, this teeming womb of royal kings,
> Fear'd by their breed, and famous by their birth,
> Renowned for their deeds as far from home,
> For Christian service and true chivalry,
> As is the sepulchre in stubborn Jewry
> Of the world's ransom, blessed Mary's son;
> This land of such dear souls, this dear dear land,
> Dear for her reputation through the world,

> Is now leas'd out—I die pronouncing it—
> Like to a tenement or pelting farm.
> (2.1.40–60)

Richard, unlike Gaunt, is invoking an ancient, sacramental magic. It is prenational, a-historical; it is the sacred, animistic bond between king and land—the *corpus mysticum* which includes and transcends both political kingdom and physical earth, as kingship includes and transcends both the king's eternal "body politic" and his personal, natural self. From this he draws the strength of his asserted belief that "Not all the water in the rough rude sea / Can wash the balm off from an anointed king." He is also invoking a lover's relationship, caressing, tender, maternal, erotic. His personifications persistently link rebellion with suggestions of sexual violation—a rape of the land:

> And when they from thy bosom pluck a flower,
> Guard it, I pray thee, with a lurking adder,
> Whose double tongue may with a mortal touch
> Throw death upon thy sovereign's enemies.
> (3.2.19–22)

Gaunt's patriotism, on the other hand, takes the form of a national pride in the virtues and achievements of an historical nation-state, its martial valor, its renown abroad, its strength and independence. It is noteworthy that his rhetoric consistently distinguishes between "land" and "state"—indeed in the famous lines, "This blessed plot, this earth, this realm, this England, / This nurse, this teeming womb of royal kings" (2.1.50–51), he makes perceptible transition from the merely native to the consciously national. That Gaunt's patriotism is anachronistic, far more Elizabethan than feudal, is less to the purpose than the perception that Richard, by contrast, is drawing upon constitutional and legal doctrine and quasi-erotic sentiment to supply the strength and confidence which "worldly men" derive from the exercise of political arts. Richard's identification of himself with his kingship and with the land he is part of and possesses constitutes the inherited and as yet untried conception of himself to which he retreats at the first crisis. It is this that circumstances will test, undermine, and finally shatter; and in the ruin of which, in the catastrophe, he will find independent individual dignity.

While Carlisle and Aumerle make their plea for the practical energies of *virtù,* Fortune and Scroop, playing the torturer by small and small, announce first the defection of the Welshmen, then the general insurrection in favor of Bolingbroke, then the execution of Bushy, Green, and the Earl of Wiltshire. Richard's reactions consist of a series of violent fluctuations between dread of worse to come and renewed hope for the power of the king's name, or the power of his uncle York. These fluctuations come to rest in a stoical attempt to withstand the tidings of calamity by reducing its significance to mere worldly loss, which can be endured with a virtuous fortitude:

> The worst is worldly loss thou canst unfold.
> Say, is my kingdom lost? Why, 'twas my care,
> And what loss is it to be rid of care?
> Strives Bolingbroke to be as great as we?
> Greater he shall not be. If he serve God,
> We'll serve Him too, and be his fellow so.
> Revolt our subjects? that we cannot mend;
> They break their faith to God as well as us.
> Cry woe, destruction, ruin, and decay—
> The worst is death, and death will have his day.
> (3.2.94–103)

But the culmination of the whole series of reactions, finely discriminated from this speech of rehearsal, is the great elegy with which Richard greets the blow of the news of his friends' death. Indeed it is this blow and its accompanying emotional perturbation (immediately following his carefully constructed stoicism) that transforms the protective pose of Christian fortitude into a great lament upon the theme of vanity. He believed his friends treacherous, and discovers their loyalty in the same breath as he discovers their death. The irony is pointed up by Scroop's equivocation: "Peace have they made with him indeed, my lord" (3.2.128). From the multiplicity of meaning radiating outward from the small word "peace" Richard's meditation upon death takes its rise. Peace of body, of mind, of conscience, the illusory peace of life—"as if this flesh which walls about our life were brass impregnable"—the peace of the grave in the hollow ground are its grand themes.

> Let's talk of graves, of worms, and epitaphs,
> Make dust our paper, and with rainy eyes
> Write sorrow on the bosom of the earth.
> Let's choose executors and talk of wills.

And yet not so—for what can we bequeath
Save our deposed bodies to the ground?
Our lands, our lives, and all, are Bollingbroke's,
And nothing can we call our own but death;
And that small model of the barren earth
Which serves as paste and cover to our bones.
For God's sake let us sit upon the ground
And tell sad stories of the death of kings:
How some have been depos'd, some vain in war,
Some haunted by the ghosts they have deposed,
Some poisoned by their wives, some sleeping kill'd,
All murthered—for within the hollow crown
That rounds the mortal temples of a king
Keeps Death his court, and there his antic sits,
Scoffing his state and grinning at his pomp,
Allowing him a breath, a little scene,
To monarchize, be fear'd, and kill with looks;
Infusing him with self and vain conceit,
As if this flesh which walls about our life
Were brass impregnable; and humour'd thus,
Comes at the last, and with a little pin
Bores through his castle wall, and farewell king!
Cover your heads, and mock not flesh and blood
With solemn reverence; throw away respect,
Tradition, form, and ceremonious duty;
For you have but mistook me all this while.
I live with bread like you, feel want,
Taste grief, need friends—subjected thus,
How can you say to me, I am a king?

(3.2.145–77)

His own deprivation, his own mortification, is the prelude to the melancholy procession of monarchs from the *Mirror for Magistrates* in all the poignant specificity of their individual deaths. But he is one of them, and the idea of the common destiny of all earthly kings is salient. The thought reaches its climax in the figure of King Death keeping his court within the hollow crown that rounds the mortal temples of a king; the metaphor articulates illusion, juxtaposing king and mock-king, king of flesh and king of shadows, in a flash of meaning *Lear* will later expand. Richard's self-awareness emerges from this dialectic of king and subject with the double puns upon "Crown" (symbol of sovereignty and mere skull) and "subjected" (made a subject and thrown down) focusing his realization of the relationship between the illusory name of king and the real nature of man, subject to elementary needs and sorrows. The very pronouns articulate the progress of this arduous shift of perspective. The speech begins with the generalizing and representative royal plural: "Let's sit," "Let's choose," "What can we bequeath," proceeds through the immensely distanced "allowing him," "infusing him," to the "me" and the "I" and the "you" of a fully exposed personal existence in the final lines.

Richard's lament yields to the scarcely concealed contempt with which the practical Carlisle urges him, "My lord, wise men ne'er sit and wail their woes," and to Aumerle's encouragement to him to remember York's force. His insight gives way to the older habitual posture. He rejects his recent outburst as an "ague fit of fear" and brashly looks forward to the winning of his own as an easy task. But the final blow is decisive. Richard's "sweet way to despair" is sweet not only because it suggests to him the consolations of an indulgence in the grief which is now all that is his own, but also because it is, in terms of a medieval *contemptus mundi*, a kind of hope. The "Kingly woe" which he resolves to obey is endued with connotations of a piety—the piety of the kingdom within—which has the power to make folly the wisdom of the world. The perspective is one which makes Bolingbroke's rise to power, crowned by vanity and haunted by guilt, a grimly ironic comment upon Carlisle's "wise men."

To call Richard's behavior here vacillation is of course to classify it correctly for practical purposes. For dramatic purposes, however, what is important is what we are enabled to infer of the nature of his ordeal and the inner strategies it gives rise to. The peripeteia which reverses his status and his situation, which makes him no king, produces self-awareness of the acutest and most poignant kind. And it would seem to be crass indeed to interpret the highly original if still somewhat stilted rendering of this self-awareness as "Richard's fatal weakness." It is often done. "He cannot bring himself to live in a world of hard actuality; the universe to him is real only as it is presented in packages of fine words"; "Aumerle tries almost roughly to recall him from his weaving of sweet, melancholy sounds . . . but he rouses himself only momentarily and then relapses into a complacent enjoyment of the sound of his own tongue." A juster analysis will surely perceive the subtlety with which the personal struggle is rendered. As he watches his power dwindle and knows himself without the innate capacity to rule, it is precisely "the hard actuality" of his situation that he perceives. And in his probing of this actuality he conceives the possibility of an alternative "address to the world" which represents another kind of sovereignty. Both impose claims upon his imagination, and each frustrates the other. "What shall the King do?" is the question that torments him. And "What shall the King do?" in circumstances in which the King's power to initiate action is lost becomes the far more radical and searching question, "What shall the King be?"

The constitutive principle throughout act 3 is that of rapid alternation, and with each thrust and counterthrust further resources of language are brought into play. Richard's appearance upon the walls of Flint castle has the imposing dignity of royal spectacle. As York points out:

> Yet looks he like a king. Behold, his eye,
> As bright as is the eagle's, lightens forth
> Controlling majesty; alack, alack for woe
> That any harm should stain so fair a show!
> (3.3.68–71)

And his address to Northumberland takes the cue with magnificent aplomb:

> We are amazed, and thus long have we stood
> To watch the fearful bending of thy knee,
> Because we thought ourselves thy lawful king:
> And if we be, how dare thy joints forget
> To pay their awful duty to our presence?
> (3.3.72–76)

In his speech the themes of legitimate descent, divine protection, the ravages of war to come are recapitulated and climaxed by one of the most moving of the recurrent image clusters:

> But ere the crown he looks for live in peace,
> Ten thousand bloody crowns of mothers' sons
> Shall ill become the flower of England's face,
> Change the complexion of her maid-pale peace
> To scarlet indignation and bedew
> Her pastures' grass with faithful English blood.
> (3.3.95–100)

The speech is in direct counterpoint to Bolingbroke's preceding threat:

> If not, I'll use the advantage of my power
> And lay the summer's dust with showers of blood
> Rain'd from the wounds of slaughtered Englishmen—
> The which, how far off from the mind of Bolingbroke
> It is such crimson tempest should bedrench
> The fresh green lap of fair King Richard's land.
> (3.3.42–47)

It should not be lost upon the sensitive ear that Richard's version of the rape of the land has the advantage in resonance, seriousness, and poetic power. The metaphor which is slighting in "the fresh green lap of fair King Richard's land" recurs in "the flower of England's face," but with an access of personal dignity in the change of bodily reference; and then is almost completely personified in "the complexion of her maid-pale peace," so that the England which will be drenched by the rain of blood is presented as the object of Richard's personal love and as a lovely object of contemplative pity. The imagery in this play is still more "poetic" than "dramatic," but an instance of the specifically poetic medium taking on a dramatic dimension is the way in which the imagery of earth, flesh, peace, blood, and growth is also used to discriminate between contrasting martial and tender modes of being. The gamut of expression thus provided constitutes the characterizing, or dramatizing, function of the imagery, and so enters into the dynamic of the play.

Richard's wholeheartedness, his role as his land's lover, gives way to bitterness at the thought of what his situation forces him to do. For this reason he overstates his accession to Bolingbroke's demands:

> Northumberland, say thus the King returns:
> His noble cousin is right welcome hither,
> And all the number of his fair demands
> Shall be accomplish'd without contradiction;
> With all the gracious utterance that thou hast
> Speak to his gentle hearing kind commends
> (3.3.121–26)

and at once plays with a repudiation of what he feels to be intolerably debasing:

> We do debase ourselves, cousin, do we not,
> To look so poorly, and to speak so fair?

> Shall we call back Northumberland and send
> Defiance to the traitor, and so die?
>
> (3.3.127–30)

The wild desire for an heroic death ("to send defiance to the traitor, and so die"), checked by Aumerle's prudence, then issues in Richard's passionate insight into the tragic discrepancy between the king's two bodies, between himself and his role, between the man that he is and the king that he ought to be.

> O that I were as great
> As is my grief, or lesser than my name!
> Or that I could forget what I have been!
> Or not remember what I must be now!
> Swell'st thou, proud heart? I'll give thee scope to beat,
> Since foes have scope to beat both thee and me.
>
> (3.3.136–41)

The previous speech, which ended with the cry, "Subjected thus / How can you say to me, I am a king?" registered his shocked realization of impotence, generated by the perception that such impotence in the face of death is the lot of common humanity. Here Richard exhibits a further stage in his awareness of himself as separate from the role history has cast upon him. The immediate result is the renunciation speech, which is flattened out of all significance if it is seen as merely another ecstasy of self-pity. The speech registers in fact a complex triple movement of feeling:

> What must the King do now? Must he submit?
> The King shall do it. Must he be depos'd?
> The King shall be contented. Must he lose
> The name of king? a God's name, let it go.
> I'll give my jewels for a set of beads;
> My gorgeous palace for a hermitage;
> My gay apparel for an almsman's gown;
> My figur'd goblets for a dish of wood;
> My scepter for a palmer's walking staff;
> My subjects for a pair of carved saints,
> And my large kingdom for a little grave,
> A little little grave, an obscure grave;
> Or I'll be buried in the King's highway,
> Some way of common trade, where subjects' feet

> May hourly trample on their sovereign's head;
> For on my heart they tread now whilst I live:
> And buried once, why not upon my head?
> Aumerle, thou weep'st (my tender-hearted cousin!),
> We'll make foul weather with despised tears;
> Our sighs and they shall lodge the summer corn,
> And make some pretty match with shedding tears?
> Or shall we play the wantons with our woes,
> As thus, to drop them still upon one place,
> Till they have fretted us a pair of graves
> Within the earth, and, therein laid—there lies
> Two kinsmen digg'd their graves with weeping eyes!
> Would not this ill do well? Well, well, I see
> I talk but idly, and you laugh at me.
> Most mighty prince, my Lord Northumberland,
> What says King Bolingbroke? Will his Majesty
> Give Richard leave to live till Richard die?
> (3.3.143–73)

The detailed, almost ritualistic specification with which he itemizes the idea of renunciation of the world suggests the intensity with which he is attempting to make a virtue of his necessity. The culminating item, however, "And my large kingdom for a little grave," initiates a collapse of this high aim. It is marvelously dramatic. The would-be saint at this point collapses into the would-be martyr, and the self-pity which overcomes him is the surest sign of an unchastened self-love, an unreadiness for and even rejection of the idea of renunciation. In the third stage of the speech this access of self-pity itself gives way to something else as the king becomes aware of Aumerle's evident emotion. His address to Aumerle, faithful king's man to the end, is indeed what it is invariably taken to be—a sentimental excursion. But it should not, I believe, be glossed exclusively to the King's disadvantage. On the contrary, if it is the verbal equivalent of the embrace of a man's arm around a friend's shoulder, it suggests the sustaining power of a gesture of sympathy, and it is in fact bracing in its effect, enabling Richard to return to the cruelty of fact: "What says King Bolingbroke? Will his Majesty / Give Richard leave to live till Richard die?" (3.3.172–73). Once again pronouns chart the spiritual progress. The royal "we" of the opening speech gave place to the titular third person used of himself at the start of the renunciation speech ("What must the king do now?"); this in turn gave way to the first person of the renunciation itself, as king was deposed into person. "Richard," royal and baptismal name, designates the now ironic identification of person and king, the two aspects of himself seen, so to speak, from without. But the descent to the base court of the deposed sun-king is rendered by the unreserved and unmitigated first person singular.

The descent to the base court marks the completion of the tragic reversal. Power has in fact passed from Richard to Bolingbroke and from now on Richard is no longer controller or initiator of events, but merely the object of Bolingbroke's designs. Though this transfer of power is not formalized until the abdication scene, it has in fact occurred; and Richard's role in act 4 is subtly different from all that has preceded it. In act 4 Richard is the victim of Bolingbroke's inexorable progress, and his protest takes the form of the inverted coronation-rite. His newly sharpened awareness of self now becomes a bitter sense of self-betrayal and consequent self-disgust. We are given our bearings upon this phase of Richard's progress by his increasing recourse to sarcasm, the only weapon of revenge, the only violence, of a weak man:

> Alack, why am I sent for to a king
> Before I have shook off the regal thoughts
> Wherewith I reign'd? I hardly yet have learn'd
> To insinuate, flatter, bow, and bend my knee.
> (4.1.162–65)

The one power he still has over Bolingbroke is the power to force him to be the witness of his violation of royalty, to force him to take responsibility, full human responsibility, for the *lèse majesté* which he sees as a replica of the ultimate sacrilege:

> Though some of you, with Pilate, wash your hands,
> Showing an outward pity—yet you Pilates
> Have here deliver'd me to my sour cross,
> And water cannot wash away your sin.
> (4.1.239–42)

Had he retired in dignified silence from the stage of history, as many of his critics apparently would have wished him to do, it would certainly have been more comfortable for the new king than the woeful pageant that we have. But the abdication scene, in which Richard stage-manages the exchange of the crown and the ritual unkinging of himself, provides the context in which the mirror episode acquires its reverberating significance.

In the mirror Richard seeks to solve the mystery of identity, of who and what he is. Truth and vanity, face and mask, self and role, substance and shadow—these dichotomies are all contained in the grand symbol of the mirror. Comparison with *Richard III* is instructive. For where Richard III watched his crooked shadow in the sun, understanding what he was in that outward figure, Richard II peruses his image in the glass, "That it may show me what a face I have / Since it is bankrupt of his majesty" (4.1.266–67). For his bafflement concerning his name and his nature has just received its most moving, passionate expression:

> Alack the heavy day,
> That I have worn so many winters out,
> And know not now what name to call myself!
> O that I were a mockery king of snow,
> Standing before the sun of Bolingbroke,
> To melt myself away in water drops!
> (4.1.257–62)

The disintegrating experience of a total breach between name and self is matched by the powerful snow-king metaphor of disintegration. The bitterness is wonderfully expressed by the transference of the sun metaphor to Bolingbroke and the transference of Bolingbroke's cold qualities to himself. Throughout the play, indeed, the orchestration of the sensuous contraries expressive of Richard's fluctuating states of mind—hot and cold, sweet and sour, pale and red, high and low, solid and melting (or brittle and liquid), harsh and tuneful—is entirely admirable.

In the shattering of the mirror is the symbol shattered, and Bolingbroke's acid comment, "The shadow of your sorrow has destroy'd the shadow of your face," extracts a yet further significance from the episode. Richard responds to the truth of Bolingbroke's pragmatism with a countertruth in which resides the grandest irony of all, did Bolingbroke but know it—the irony of the inner reality of anguish and guilt of which the pomp and power of kingship's outer action is but the shadow:

> 'Tis very true, my grief lies all within,
> And these external manners of laments

> Are merely shadows to the unseen grief
> That swells with silence in the tortur'd soul.
> There lies the substance.
>
> (4.1.295–99)

The sequence of scenes which runs from 3.4 to 5.1 is of absorbing interest from the point of view taken in these pages, that is to say from the point of view of the discovery of Shakespeare's tragic form. The act division reflects the fall-rise plot construction: the garden scene, coming immediately after the surrender at Flint castle, provides a suitable comment upon Richard's government of his kingdom, and therefore signals the change of regime which is to follow. Act 4 initiates the rise to supreme power of Bolingbroke and begins therefore with his examination of Bagot and the renewed confrontation between the rival barons, echoing act 1. Act 4 ends with Richard's abdication and the plans for Bolingbroke's coronation, leaving for act 5 the final moves in the transfer of power: Richard's incarceration in the Tower, the queen's exile to France, Aumerle's conspiracy, which presents Bolingbroke with his first treason (foreshadowing things to come), and the death of Richard. Act division therefore faithfully reflects the construction of the play in terms of the overthrow of Richard's legitimate monarchy and the usurpation of Bolingbroke. But an eye trained by Shakespeare's later practice perceives at once that both 3.4, the gardener scene, and 5.1, the leave-taking scene between Richard and his weeping queen, in fact contain the sort of material that was to become, in the later tragedies, Shakespeare's characteristic fourth phase. This is the phase in which the tragic experience is rendered by some form of despair or repudiation of his world on the part of the protagonist, and modified by bearings taken from a vantage point outside and beyond the hero. It is the phase in which the great fall is wryly domesticated, and lit, so to speak, by transverse beams of pathos and irony. Both the pathos and the irony are methods for presenting the heroic image refracted in the medium provided by the viewpoint of simple, often anonymous, common folk.

In *Richard II* these resources are not deployed to the full as they will be later, where they are wonderfully juxtaposed and counterpointed so as to make the richest harmonic effects possible. Here they remain discrete and relatively unimpressive. The Gardener, effectively elegiac, is too explicitly allegorical for his comment upon "what men do, not knowing what they do" to have the maximum impact of dramatic irony. Later Shakespeare will transpose the key of such comment into the inspired fool's wisdom of gnomic gravediggers, or the earthy wisdom of an Emilia, while the contrapuntal darkened vision of Richard, "A king of beasts, indeed—if aught but beasts, / I had been still a happy king of men" (5.1.35–36), becomes "the wren goes to 't" and "a dog's obeyed in office" of Lear. In *Richard II* the content of the darkened vision has not been so objectively grounded in the very action of the play; nor has it the coordinated, accumulated reverberation of Lear's black apocalypse. In *Richard II* the ceremony and policy which veil human savagery are not rent entirely asunder as they are in *Lear.* Evil is fully accounted for in terms of political expediency, political error, political opportunism. Faces and fortunes are shattered, but the protagonists are not cut to the very brains. In *Lear* evil bursts all bounds and creates a vertiginous abyss. Nevertheless in Richard's somewhat decorative "lamentable tale," with which even "the senseless brands will sympathize" (5.1.40–50), is the germ of "I should e'en die with pity to see another thus"; and in his "I am sworn brother, sweet, / To grim necessity" is foreshadowed "I am bound upon a wheel of fire, that mine own tears / Do scald like molten lead."

In neither Richard's case nor Lear's is the hero's tragedy complete at this stage. The inexorable process that forces a man to face the worst the fates hold in store for him comes after he has entertained a delusive hope of accommodation with what he takes, in his ignorance, to be the worst. This total knowledge of the worst constitutes the tragic catastrophe. It is, in a sense, Aristotle's anagnorisis taken to its furthest limit and unfolded in its fullest relatedness to what has gone before. In the final turn of the tragedy the Shakespearean tragic hero offers us more than a repentant acknowledgment of his own share of responsibility for the events. He may do this. But he does very much more than this. He bears witness to his own personal self-definition, to some distinctive form of human integrity, some inalienable individual perception of value of which his life is the gauge. The prison scenes at Pomfret perfectly illustrate the process.

The first part of the soliloquy, in which Richard sets his brain and his soul to breed thoughts, provides striking confirmation of what we have already discovered to have been dramatized in the play: Richard's oscillation between "the better sort" of thought and the worse; between the conflicting impulses which have constituted his struggle to achieve and maintain either virtue or *virtù,* the inner or the outer kingdom:

The better sort,
As thoughts of things divine, are intermix'd
With scruples, and do set the word itself
Against the word,
As thus: "Come, little ones"; And then again,
"It is as hard to come as for a camel
To thre- ' the postern of a small needle's eye."
Thoughts tending to ambition, they do plot
Unlikely wonders: how these vain weak nails
May tear a passage through the flinty ribs
Of this hard world, my ragged prison walls;
And for they cannot, die in their own pride.
Thoughts tending to content flatter themselves
That they are not the first of fortune's slaves,
Nor shall not be the last—like silly beggars
Who, sitting in the stocks, refuge their shame,
That many have and others must sit there;
And in this thought they find a kind of ease,
Bearing their own misfortunes on the back
Of such as have before endur'd the like.
(5.5.11–30)

Thoughts of things divine are undermined by his doubts of his capacity for them. Thoughts of grand defiance die in their own impotent pride. The elaborate figure in which the brain is female to the soul is Shakespeare's way of rendering what is actually the first passage of formal introspection in the play. The result of Richard's thus turning his eyes inward is the detachment with which he views his own attempts at resignation. These are thoughts which merely "flatter," which seek "a kind of ease" by the attempt to mitigate pain through dissipation in the thought of others' misfortunes. But in no thought can he find rest. These reflections bring him back to the great theme of role versus self, and to the ultimate nothing that awaits all men:

Thus play I in one person many people,
And none contented. Sometimes am I king,
Then treasons make me wish myself a beggar,
And so I am. Then crushing penury
Persuades me I was better when a king;
Then am I king'd again, and by and by
Think that I am unking'd by Bolingbroke,

And straight am nothing. But what e'er I be,
Nor I, nor any man that but man is,
With nothing shall be pleas'd, till he be eas'd
With being nothing.

(5.5.31–41)

"What, in ill thoughts again?" an Edgar might well have said; and indeed the transition to the idea of discord in the soul is implicit in the speech even before the music symbolizes it. The music, whose broken time apparently breaks into his train of thought, in reality focuses it. The idea of time broken, musically and metaphorically, in the music of men's lives, has the clearest relevance to his preoccupation with his own mismanagement of opportunities. And with the music, Richard's musing summary of his progress of the soul takes on a new urgency and energy of analysis:

How sour sweet music is
When time is broke, and no proportion kept!
So is it in the music of men's lives.
And here have I the daintiness of ear
To check time broke in a disordered string;
But for the concord of my state and time,
Had not an ear to hear my true time broke:
I wasted time, and now doth time waste me;
For now hath time made me his numb'ring clock;

. . . .

But my time
Runs posting on in Bolingbroke's proud joy,
While I stand fooling here, his Jack of the clock.

(5.5.42–60)

It may not be without relevance to note that Marvell, whose "Horatian Ode" is in many ways a mid-century reincarnation of the drama of Richard II, uses the image of the Jack-of-the-clock in his "The First Anniversary of Cromwell's Return from Ireland" for the merely hereditary kings who are not masters of time and men's minds:

Thus (Image-like) an useless time they tell,
And with vain scepter, strike the hourly Bell;
No more contribute to the state of Things,
Than wooden Heads unto the Viols strings.

(ll. 41–44)

The image has a Machiavellian resonance. In his letter to Soderini, "On Fortune and the Times," Machiavelli expounds the doctrine that a man may hope to master Fortune—the concatenation of forces which the Prince faces—by *virtù* properly understood and practiced:

> And therefore the cautious man, when it is time to turn adventurous, does not know how to do it, hence he is ruined; . . . For my part I consider that it is better to be adventurous than cautious, because fortune is a woman, and if you wish to keep her under it is necessary to beat and ill use her; and it is seen that she allows herself to be mastered by the adventurous rather than those who go to work more coldly.

The point I wish to emphasize is one that is not usually stressed: the latter half of Richard's monologue is very definitely in the direction of the world. Richard may be a wiser and better man at the end of the play than he was at the beginning, though much of what he learns the great commonplaces of all times teach. But struggle as he may towards resignation or renunciation, the unregenerate bent and drag of his nature is toward his lost royalty, and no divine thoughts have succeeded in sweetening the sour taste of deposition, the bitter realization of what he has lost and of what he has allowed himself to become.

What happens between the entrance of the groom and the end needs for its full understanding the "reflector" scenes between York and Aumerle which immediately precede Pomfret, and to which I have previously referred. York has been throughout the very image of a divided spirit. He remonstrates with Richard in his brother's and his nephew's defense, yet he sharply reproves Northumberland for want of reverence to the King at Flint Castle. He is torn between kinsmen, between loyalty and justice:

> Th' one is my sovereign, whom both my oath
> And duty bids defend; th' other again
> Is my kinsman, whom the King hath wrong'd,
> Whom conscience and my kindred bids to right.
> (2.2.112–15)

He can choose no path which will annul the contrary alternative. While he is the spokesman of compassion for Richard in his description of the well-graced royal actor leaving the stage,

men's eyes
Did scowl on Richard. No man cried "God save him!"
No joyful tongue gave him his welcome home,
But dust was thrown upon his sacred head.
(5.2.27–30)

the description prefaces his assertion that "To Bolingbroke are we sworn subjects now." The revelation of Aumerle's conspiracy in favor of the deposed but after all still legitimate king produces an extremity of reaction in York that has puzzled commentators. I believe it fruitful to see the York episode as dramatically functional, as preliminary to Richard's death to which it points by contrast. For what is enacted in the conspiracy scene is the total breakdown of the man, his complete loss of inner coherence, the disintegration of his identity as man and father. He is so eroded by his inner warfare with inescapable treason that he can deliver his own son to the sword. The violence of his outburst in the teeth of the impassioned voice of nature in his wife's pleading is evidence of the breakdown. If the whole episode is a replica in little of the fate of the kingdom delivered over to civil strife, and an anticipation of Henry IV's problem with his wayward son, York's part in it at least is the immediate prelude to the recovery of self-possession by the dispossessed king. For this is the final outcome of the catastrophe.

The encounter with the groom and the story of the horse recall Richard to himself and renew his fighting spirit and his power of self-assertion. The defiant reflex of the will is produced by the combination of the simple affection and loyalty of the groom, which makes a "brooch in this all-hating world," and the defection of roan Barbary—potent chivalric symbol of martial valour, and, proudly carrying Bolingbroke, exquisitely fitting symbol of the King's eclipse:

So proud that Bolingbroke was on his back!
That jade hath eat bread from my royal hand;
This hand hath made him proud with clapping him.
Would he not stumble? Would he not fall down,
Since pride must have a fall, and break the neck
Of that proud man that did usurp his back?
Forgiveness, horse! Why do I rail on thee,
Since thou, created to be aw'd by man,
Wast born to bear? I was not made a horse,

> And yet I bear a burden like an ass,
> Spurr'd, gall'd, and tir'd by jauncing Bolingbroke.
> (5.5.84–94)

"I was not made a horse"—it is an unexpected turn, therefore splendidly expressive: "The devil take Henry of Lancaster, and thee! / Patience is stale, and I am weary of it." Richard, dispossessed of crown, queen, kingdom, hereditary role, and even the lordly creature that bore him on its back, reduced to something as near as the impure tragedy of the histories will get to unaccommodated man, finds in himself undreamt-of resources of willed defiance and sells his life dearly, in kingly fashion. It is the simplest kind of catharsis, a restoration of a lost heroic value. But it enables Exton to salute the sovereign that he kills with "As full of valour as of royal blood." King Richard is eclipsed, but the fact, or the dream, or the image of truly royal prowess, finally redemptive of folly and vanity, survives.

This Royal Throne Unkinged

Maynard Mack, Jr.

Richard II tells the very simple story of the deposition and death of the last Angevin king. The first act sets the situation as the king exiles his cousin, Bolingbroke, because of a mysterious dispute relating to the murder of their famous uncle, Thomas of Woodstock; the first scene of the next act supplies the motive for Bolingbroke's return, when Richard seizes his inheritance. The rest of the play shows Bolingbroke rising and Richard falling until the deposed king is murdered at Pomfret Castle.

Many of Shakespeare's plays tell of the death of kings, some of two or more deaths in one play, but no other play deals so thoroughly and exclusively with the subject—politically conceived. There is hardly a scene that does not cast its political weight directly on Richard's shoulders; not a single character in the play remains isolated from the central political action. Nor are there the many probing soliloquies and supernatural elements that in *Hamlet* and *Macbeth,* for example, expand the central action of killing the king to a general philosophic and intensely metaphoric concern. In its fundamental outlines, therefore, *Richard II* is above all a play about political struggle.

To say only this, however, is to leave out what is most interesting in the play: the background of images in front of which, and often in terms of which, the conflict is waged. This is what I have called

From *Killing the King: Three Studies in Shakespeare's Tragic Structure.* © 1973 by Yale University. Yale University Press, 1973.

[elsewhere] the structure for king killing, the imaginative setting in which the action occurs. To this setting I now turn.

Gaunt's deathbed eulogy of England, the royal throne of kings, has always stood out from the rest of the play—partly because it is a remarkable piece of writing, and partly because it is carefully set in a context calculated to give it maximum resonance. Richard, fresh from having stopped the combat between Bolingbroke and Mowbray, receives the news that Gaunt is dying. As he leaves the stage with the brutal comment "Pray God we may make haste and come too late!" (1.4.64), he and his companions are replaced by representatives of a different world: "*Enter* John of Gaunt *sick, with the* Duke of York." Gaunt asks:

> Will the king come that I may breathe my last
> In wholesome counsel to his unstaid youth?
> . . . .
> O, but they say the tongues of dying men
> Inforce attention like deep harmony.
>
> (2.1.1–6)

Gone here are Richard's confident jests and nasty ridicule, and in their place is a helpless question followed by a different kind of confidence, the quiet confidence of age that has seen much. Though Gaunt is physically weak and politically helpless, he feels himself filled with the spiritual power of the "prophet new inspir'd" (2.1.31). He speaks a formal, frequently rhymed verse that we have heard before in the ceremonious accusations of treason. But there is a new note of rhetorical pattern, sententiousness, and adage-making. As Gaunt talks with York, he piles up pithy phrases as if he were seeking the precisely correct statement.

> Where words are scarce they are seldom spent in vain,
> For they breathe truth that breathe their words in pain.
> He that no more must say is listened more
> Than they whom youth and ease have taught to glose;
> More are men's ends mark'd than their lives before.
> The setting sun, and music at the close,
> As the last taste of sweets, is sweetest last,
> Writ in remembrance more than things long past.
>
> (2.1.7–14)

Or else he repeats proverbial wisdom, apparently willing it to be true through the cumulative power of the rhetoric.

His rash fierce blaze of riot cannot last.
For violent fires soon burn out themselves;
Small showers last long, but sudden storms are short;
He tires betimes that spurs too fast betimes;
With eager feeding food doth choke the feeder;
Light vanity, insatiate cormorant,
Consuming means, soon preys upon itself.
(2.1.33–39)

Then suddenly in the next line the tone changes, and the rhetoric, though no less formal, breaks free of its didacticism into the rhythm of pure hymn.

This royal throne of kings, this scept'red isle,
This earth of majesty, this seat of Mars,
This other Eden, demi-paradise,
This fortress built by Nature for herself
Against infection and the hand of war,
This happy breed of men, this little world,
This precious stone set in the silver sea,
Which serves it in the office of a wall,
Or as a moat defensive to a house,
Against the envy of less happier lands;
This blessed plot, this earth, this realm, this England,
This nurse, this teeming womb of royal kings,
Fear'd by their breed, and famous by their birth,
Renowned for their deeds as far from home,
For Christian service and true chivalry,
As is the sepulchre in stubborn Jewry
Of the world's ransom, blessed Mary's Son.
(2.1.40–56)

These lines place England in an optimistic but complex perspective. The heavy emphasis on royalty shows kingship to be the central issue of Gaunt's thoughts, as of the play in general. England's insularity is also stressed and this underscores both the precariousness of its natural and political situation and its symbolic status as a nation isolated from lesser breeds and destined to stand or fall alone. Two further aspects of Gaunt's words are especially important. One consists in the suprapolitical images which tie his thoughts about England's kings to a long-standing natural and religious tradition. From "Eden, demi-paradise" Gaunt's thought flows on uninterruptedly to "This fortress built by Nature for herself." Two traditions, one Christian, one possibly but not necessarily pagan, are here blended to mark England as the choice of both God and Nature. The Christian tradition is picked up ten lines later in "Christian service" and "blessed Mary's Son," while the close connection with Nature underlies the image of England as "This nurse, this teeming womb."

The idea that brings the whole speech to its climax is that of a Christian heroic service. It is, we notice, a service rugged, fierce, and energetic, based on a tough-minded conception of the world and of England's place in it. In Gaunt's view England is great because of its great strength both at home and abroad. "This other Eden" is first of all "this seat of Mars," a fortress; its insularity serves it as a "wall," a "moat" against assault. It is an order fiercely defended. Its fame is based not on its justice or its culture, as the modern audience might prefer, but on its deeds of strength, specifically in the Crusades—though these Crusades no doubt serve here as expressions of all three national virtues. So long as its kings are *feared,* the precious jewel is safe. Such is the England Gaunt praises, the kind of Christian service he remembers. And it is from this exalted state that England is falling.

> This land of such dear souls, this dear dear land,
> Dear for her reputation through the world,
> Is now leas'd out—I die pronouncing it—
> Like to a tenement or pelting farm.
> England, bound in with the triumphant sea,
> Whose rocky shore beats the envious siege
> Of wat'ry Neptune, is now bound in with shame,
> With inky blots and rotten parchment bonds;
> That England, that was wont to conquer others,
> Hath made a shameful conquest of itself.
>
> (2.1.57–66)

These may be the words of a weak and dying man, but there is nothing weak or helpless in their conception of the world. Even Neptune is apprehended as an "envious" attacking force to be resisted. And now the rugged power, the spare frugality suggested even in Gaunt's name (ll. 73–83), is being destroyed from the inside by foolish waste and shameful bonds that commit England's revenues to favorites of the king. The harmony of discipline that made this other Eden both God's and Nature's chosen home is threatened by the discord created and allowed by a willful misled king. Richard is a king but no Mars renowned for his deeds; he is Christian but has failed in "service"—because he has also failed in strength.

What Gaunt says in this speech and the lost ideals he stands for inform the whole play. From its very first line he is "Old John of Gaunt, time-honoured Lancaster," who like an ancient landmark chiefly functions to measure change. Later in the first scene he loyally obeys his king in trying to calm the angry disputants, and in the second scene with the Duchess of Gloucester, he reveals the yet fiercer loyalty that has kept him obedient to Richard though he knows the king is responsible for his brother Woodstock's death. His manner of refusing the Duchess's demand that he avenge her reveals a firmly established hierarchy of loyalties and priorities, surviving from a world now all but gone. He rates the fact that Gloucester was his brother above the widow's "exclaims" (1.2.2), but rates his duty to Richard higher still because of his supreme duty to God, whose deputy Richard is.

> Put we our quarrel to the will of heaven,
> Who, when they see the hours ripe on earth,
> Will rain hot vengeance on offenders' heads.
> (1.2.6–8)

His words may appear at first evasive and inadequate to the situation in the light of the angry charges of treason in the preceding scene, in which all parties have invoked heavenly support. But Gaunt's conservative faith cannot be rejected as merely "poignant impossibility" unless we are prepared to ignore a good deal of evidence. The necessary criticism of his view is already implicit in the Duchess's comment "Call it not patience, Gaunt, it is despair" (1.2.29), and Shakespeare provides no easy judgment between the two claims. Like the royal widows in *3 Henry VI* and *Richard III,* she invokes images of the specific natural womb that bore both the murdered man and Gaunt (1.2.22), while his thoughts tend toward God and the more general teeming womb that bears England's kings.

When Richard arrives to see Gaunt die, the old man is quick to warn him in clear terms of what is happening to England, though, in the king's presence, his style changes significantly. The prophetic rhetoric of his earlier hymn to the royal throne of kings takes second place to an ironic wit that seems to come, with Richard, from the preceding scene of jests against "high Herford" (1.4.3). But the substance of his address is the same: "Thy deathbed is no lesser than thy land" (2.1.95). Apart from one indirect mention of his son's banishment (ll. 79–81), his thoughts are filled solely with the health of England and the potential greatness of both country and ruler. In this vein, he evokes his memories of Edward III and the Black Prince:

> O, spare me not, my brother Edward's son,
> For that I was his father Edward's son.
>
> (2.1.124–25)

And York evokes similar memories as soon as news of Gaunt's death is announced.

> I am the last of noble Edward's sons,
> Of whom thy father, Prince of Wales, was first.
> In war was never lion rag'd more fierce,
> In peace was never gentle lamb more mild,
> Than was that young and princely gentleman.
> His face thou hast, for even so look'd he,
> Accomplish'd with the number of thy hours;
> But when he frown'd it was against the French,
> And not against his friends.
>
> (2.1.171–79)

Here is an image of the good prince that hovers in the background of every scene. It is a picture of energy and also of order. It is an ideal of rigorous balance between opposites, not necessarily subtle but reliable and restrained. In this prince, as in imagined England-Eden, lamb and lion lie down together.

The view of kingship held by Gaunt and York, and, we discover later, by Carlisle, corresponds, in one way of understanding it, to the very order of the universe. As Tillyard, C. S. Lewis, and so many others have shown, kingship was simply another dimension of the general hierarchical order that prevailed in the Elizabethan world-picture. York voices the pure doctrine when he warns Richard that rebellion in one area will cause trouble in others.

> Take Herford's rights away, and take from time
> His charters, and his customary rights;
> Let not to-morrow then ensue to-day:
> Be not thyself. For how art thou a king
> But by fair sequence and succession?
>
> (2.1.195–99)

Three vastly different areas of experience are here linked. Inheritance, time, and kingship are all presented as analogical. As one critic [Sigurd Burckhardt] has described this kind of thinking, "Everything was like everything else; beneath the diversity in degree there was a remarkable likeness in kind." York exploits this view as a means of ordering and imaginatively controlling the rapidly changing facts that confront him. Spotting Richard on the walls of Flint Castle, he says:

> Yet looks he like a king. Behold, his eye,
> As bright as is the eagle's, lightens forth
> Controlling majesty; alack, alack for woe
> That any harm should stain so fair a show!
> (3.3.68–71)

The heavy use of simile and the word "show" may hint at an imaginable breakdown in the analogies by which the king can appropriately be signified as God on earth, or the eagle among birds, the lion among mammals, the diamond among stones, and so on. But the lines alert us also to the whole implicit structure of royal correspondences that run throughout the play and define one conception of kingship.

This structure of correspondences emphasizes primarily unity and power. On the highest level the king is seen as closely linked with God, as "God's substitute, / His deputy anointed in His sight" (1.2.37–38):

> the figure of God's majesty,
> His captain, steward, deputy elect,
> Anointed, crowned, planted many years.
> (4.1.125–27)

God's aid is invoked lest "in a Christian climate souls refin'd / Should show so heinous, black, obscene a deed" (4.1.130–31) as killing his vicegerent. "Stirr'd up by God thus boldly for his king" (4.1.133), Carlisle utters the famous prophecy of the disastrous effects for England if the divine and natural hierarchy is disturbed.

Richard himself of course relies on the connection between God and king throughout. He claims that "God for his Richard hath in heavenly pay / A glorious angel" (3.2.60–61); he asks Northumberland to "show us the hand of God / That hath dismiss'd us from our stewardship" (3.3.77–78); he asserts that his "master, God omnipotent" (3.3.85) will prepare armies of pestilence in his defense. In the deposition scene he explicitly calls upon God to pardon the oaths that had been broken in the transfer of power from old to new king. His frequent comparisons of himself to Christ in the hands of Pilate and Judas further enlarge the web of divine connections that in this play surrounds the idea of the king. Even at the moment when the nature of Bolingbroke's demands is at last revealed, Northumberland continues to invoke the sanctity of the royal person: "The King of heaven forbid our lord the king / Should so with civil and uncivil arms / Be rush'd upon" (3.3.101–3).

The imagery of relationship between God and king is paralleled on a less specifically Christian level by imagery of relationship between the king and Nature. The most obvious imagery of this sort, as many critics have pointed out, is the traditional comparison of sun and king which Richard frequently makes, calling himself "the searching eye of heaven" (3.2.37), describing how thieves and robbers who thrive during the night "Stand bare . . . trembling at themselves" (3.2.46) when the "day"—both sun and king—dawns. Other images implying sympathy between the political and natural worlds abound. Richard imagines a powerful conspiracy of the elements to help him in the face of danger (3.2.4–26). He animates the earth, expressing sympathy for the pain she suffers from the hooves of rebels' horses. He calls upon the earth to oppose to Bolingbroke her spiders, toads, nettles, adders. He supposes that her very stones, like the dragon's teeth in the Jason story, will turn to "armed men" to protect his throne. When Bolingbroke says at their first encounter "be he the fire, I'll be the yielding water" (3.3.58), the comparison sets the conflict of king and rebel in a context of hierarchic natural elements that comments tacitly on Bolingbroke's own soon-to-be-accomplished inversion of hierarchy in the human world.

When the Welsh captain alludes to withering bay trees and falling meteors as foreshadowing Richard's doom, his words take us again into that web of sympathies which secretly embrace the anointed king. The Queen's striking description of her husband—"Ah, thou, the model where old Troy did stand" (5.1.11)—looks in a similar direction. Though it emphasizes his fallen state, it does so in an image genealogical, architectural, geographical even, that glorifies and magnifies his mysterious significance. The conception of London as "New Troy" lies of course behind her conceit, but into it seems to flow also some of the feelings that the Renaissance had absorbed from Virgil about the ruined city beside the sea that fathered Rome and thereby civilization.

In this particular play, which comes early in his career and rather quickly on the heels of his earlier historical tetralogy, it is not easy to exaggerate the role that Shakespeare's imagination assigns to these and other standard fixtures in the lore of kingship. Richard asserts his power, for example, by comparing himself to the king of the beasts, "lions make leopards tame" (1.1.174), and his Queen urges him on reminding him that "the lion dying thrusteth forth his paw / And wounds the earth" (5.1.29–30). Later he discovers that his horse Barbary has betrayed him by not protesting against a new rider, the usurping Bolingbroke, and exclaims: "Would he not stumble? would he not fall down?" (5.5.87). But he catches himself: "Forgiveness, horse!" (l. 90). The episode is revealing. It tells us something about Richard, who has obviously gained in self-knowledge, for while his questions presuppose the sympathetic support of nature, his answer recognizes that he has forfeited such support precisely by not behaving like a king, or even like a man.

> Forgiveness, horse! why do I rail on thee,
> Since thou, created to be aw'd by man,
> Wast born to bear? I was not made a horse,
> And yet I bear a burthen like an ass,
> Spurr'd, gall'd and tir'd by jauncing Bolingbroke.
> (5.5.90–94)

Perhaps the passage also tells us something about Shakespeare. "Forgiveness, horse!" is a phrase that today actors find themselves inclined to muffle, cut, or throw away. Its appeal to an equine moral sense touches modern risibilities. To the extent that the effect was different for Shakespeare and his Elizabethan audience, as we have reason to believe it was, it must have been made so by the seriousness with which the system of sympathetic forces joining natural, human, and divine could still be taken. At another level, the dogged loyalty of the groom who appears in Richard's cell for no other reason than "To look upon my sometimes master's face" (5.5.75) makes the same point. Even in prison, the king's face merits a pilgrimage.

Most important, however, of all the dimensions of ideal kingship is not the divinity that doth hedge it, but its capacity to maintain a stable, just, and energetic order through ordinary political acumen and force. Carlisle seconds Richard's faith in divine support but urges too that "the means that heaven yields must be imbrac'd" (3.2.29). The brief lyric glimpse we get of Mowbray later in the play celebrates his having fought "Many a time . . . For Jesu Christ in glorious Christian field" (4.1.92–93), only after which, "toil'd with works of war," he "retir'd himself / To Italy" to die (ll. 96–97). Similarly, in York's memories the Black Prince is "that young Mars of men" (2.3.100). In his own image of himself, Richard was "not born to sue, but to command" (1.1.196); "the king's name" is "twenty thousand names" (3.2.85); "Ten thousand bloody crowns of mothers' sons" (3.3.96) must stain the land before his throne can be usurped. In short, to borrow a phrase from the Duchess of York, the efficient king who roots out traitors and resolves civil and familial strife is "A god on earth" (5.3.134). When he is less than this it is because "The king is not himself, but basely led / By flatterers" (2.1.241–42), and the country must "shake off [its] slavish yoke, . . . And make high majesty look like itself" again (2.1.291–95). As we saw earlier, only in the king's own name can the king himself be uncrowned.

In all these forms, Shakespeare keeps the official lore of kingship before us throughout the play. It is not, of course, *all* that he keeps before us, for there are crosscurrents of irony and qualification on every page, which will be noticed in their proper place. All that needs to be said here is that though these crosscurrents qualify the system of references at which we have been looking, they do not cancel them out. In poetry, no strand of meaning ever wholly disappears however much it may be colored by other elements in the context. Hence, though the official lore I have just now summarized, the idea of a divine, natural, and human axis with the king its center, is often enough objected to in the play, and either undercut with ridicule or overlaid with disbelief, it is never entirely obliterated from our apprehension of the play's imaginative meaning. Though it fails to find again so clear a spokesman as the dying Gaunt, it survives him to become, in its turn, an ironic comment on a new kind of kingship. To put this matter more succinctly, all the images and actions of kingship we have traced, the network of correspondences and dynamic energies, establish a definition of kingship which, for want of a better term, we might call nostalgic. It is a definition filled with imaginative power, but embodied primarily in warriors either dead or dying. Like the Golden Age it seems most visible when it is moving away, into the past.

Syntax as Rhetoric in *Richard II*

Stephen Booth

In its first scene *Richard II* is a frustrating play to listen to, and much of the frustration is syntactically evoked. By scene 3, when an audience seems about to see scene 1 replayed in a decisive, efficient, and satisfying way, King Richard himself has become the source of our frustration; and some of that frustration is also syntactically based. When Richard returns from Ireland in act 3, scene 2, nothing about him has changed but his syntax; from there to the end of the play his syntax is straightforward, and its straightforwardness colors our responses to him.

Before I set about demonstrating the justice of the foregoing assertions, let me make an obvious distinction easily ignored in criticism, a distinction between characters whom audiences recognize as somehow pleasant or unpleasant and characters who are actually pleasing or displeasing to an audience. York points to a related distinction in a simile in act 5:

> As in a theatre the eyes of men,
> After a well-graced actor leaves the stage,
> Are idly bent on him that enters next,
> Thinking his prattle to be tedious,
> Even so, or with much more contempt, men's eyes
> Did scowl on gentle Richard.
>
> (5.2.23–28)

From *Mosaic: A Journal for the Comparative Study of Literature and Ideas* 10, no. 3 (Spring 1977). © 1977 by the University of Manitoba Press.

The dimension that accidents of theatrical casting thrust upon our responses to characters superimposes itself on two that are already inherent in any dramatic text. Often the two dimensions coincide: Juliet is charming in the story of *Romeo and Juliet*, and she actually charms us, us as audience; we are always glad to listen to Juliet. Just as often, however, our responses as theatrical consumers coexist—but do not at all coincide—with our rational estimate of a character. For instance, Juliet's nurse is, as everyone always and rightly says, a garrulous bore, one who frustrates the progress of her scenes and of her companions on stage. On the other hand, we, as audience, are glad to listen to the nurse. Polonius is a similar example. What I am doing here might be clarified if I flirt with the heresy of using the word "person" to designate a character as we understand him to be and reserving the word "character" to designate a stage figure *as* stage figure—a theatrical commodity to be savored. Iago and Macbeth are thus bad people but good characters. Malcolm is a good person, but—by virtue of his perversely paced style of discourse in *Macbeth* 4.3—a bad character. (Ask any actor if he would like to play Malcolm; he would not like to play Malcolm.)

In the third scene of *Richard II* we seem to have come to the trial by combat that never materialized in act 1, scene 1. The audience hears a crisp reprise of the beginning of scene 1 (where it took Richard six lines to say "Old John of Gaunt . . . / Hast thou . . . / Brought hither Henry Hereford"). Now the Lord Marshal opens scene 3 in an echo of the earlier question: "My Lord Aumerle, is Harry Hereford armed?" Six lines into this scene, we are all ready to go: "Why, then the champions are prepared, and stay / For nothing but his majesty's approach." His majesty enters immediately, followed quickly by both combatants. A hundred lines of ceremony later, the second herald announces that Mowbray stands there "Attending but the signal to begin" (1.3.116). "Sound trumpets, and set forward, combatants," says the Marshal and then, almost in the same breath, "Stay! The king hath thrown his warder down." Richard has frustrated both the action and the audience. We are not to see the much advertised combat—or even a stageable substitute for it. Richard has become a liability to the audience, a source of theatrical irritation to the audience *as* audience.

As scene 3 continues, Richard will make similarly decisive use of his authority similarly to diminish or deny the decisiveness of the action: when Bolingbroke and Mowbray have taken their leaves and Richard calls them back; when Richard reduces Bolingbroke's term of banishment; and, most pervasively, in the frustrating sentence structure that draws his speech acts out to ineffectuality.

I want to talk about Richard's syntax in scene 3, but first I want to go back to scene 1 and establish the difference between that generally frustrating scene and scene 3, in which Richard himself is the sole and direct cause of theatrical dissatisfaction.

Scene 1 is a kind of emblem of the whole of *Richard II,* of the whole theatrical construct. The scene is, in effect, replayed over the whole length of the play—first in scene 3, again in 4.1 (when Aumerle is challenged), and, in parody form, by the York family in 5.3. Not getting to the point, not letting actions and situations finish so that new ones can follow, is of the essence of this play—an exploitable necessity of the unavoidable fact that any audience comes to this play knowing that its event will be Bolingbroke's overthrow of Richard. Scene 1 is not only emblematic by virtue of its unconcluded action and the inconclusiveness it gets from being repeated later, but also in its own internal physics and—in particular—in its syntactic physics. The scene pushes each member of its audience toward being his own Pierce Exton—impatient to hear a decisive assertion in a muddle of indecisive verbal gestures.

With the notable and rhetorically meaningful exception of Gaunt, everyone in scene 1 is inclined to invert his syntax, to stretch it, and to take any opportunity for forcing parentheses between subjects and verbs and between verbs and objects. For example, these two "I say that" constructions in a twenty-one-line speech by Bolingbroke:

> Besides I say, and will in battle prove—
> Or here, or elsewhere to the furthest verge
> That ever was surveyed by English eye—
> That all the treasons for these eighteen years.
> (1.1.92–95)

> Further I say, and further will maintain,
> Upon his bad life to make all this good,
> That he did plot the Duke of Gloucester's death.
> (ll. 98–100)

And this, from Mowbray:

> my fair name,
> Despite of death that lives upon my grave,

To dark dishonor's use thou shalt not have.
(ll. 167–69)

If "hard to understand" were not an idiom meaning "puzzling," I would say that sentences like those are hard to understand. However, there is nothing puzzling about them. They are more literally "hard to understand"; understanding them is trying—they are hard to listen to. One's mind holds a vital element while the sentence wanders elegantly toward predication.

Scene 1 is also hard to listen to because its characters regularly respond to questions and demands in syntaxes that—though clear enough in intent, and thus serviceable—do not mesh with the syntaxes they follow. For instance, when Richard says "What does thou object / Against the Duke of Norfolk, Thomas Mowbray?" Bolingbroke sets off in orderly fashion on an answer removed from the question by an irrelevantly focused gesture:

First—heaven be the record to my speech!—
In the devotion of a subject's love,
Tend'ring the precious safety of my prince
And free from other, misbegotten hate,
Come I appellant to this princely presence.
(ll. 30–34)

When at last he turns to—and cautiously approaches—the point, he answers Richard's question by demonstration—by charging Mowbray:

Now, Thomas Mowbray, do I turn to thee,
And mark my greeting well; for what I speak
My body shall make good upon this earth
Or my divine soul answer it in heaven.
Thou art a traitor and a miscreant,
Too good to be so, and too bad to live,
Since the more fair and crystal is the sky,
The uglier seem the clouds that in it fly.
Once more, the more to aggravate the note,
With a foul traitor's name stuff I thy throat
And wish, so please my sovereign, ere I move,
What my tongue speaks my right-drawn sword may prove.
(ll. 35–46)

The question is answered, but not in its own syntactical terms, not in a construction like "I charge that Mowbray is, or did, so-and-so." The scene is easy enough to follow, but we follow it without a syntactic thread from point to point and speech to speech.

Scene 1 shows us a lot about Richard, and we like none of what we learn (for instance, he punishes Bolingbroke and Mowbray by ordering the trial by combat he is punishing them for demanding). However, until scene 3 we have nothing against Richard as theatrical character, as potential source of theatrical satisfaction. What Richard says and the way he says it make him contemptible, but he is entertaining. For instance:

> Let's purge this choler without letting blood.
> This we prescribe, though no physician;
> Deep malice makes too deep incision.
> Forget, forgive; conclude and be agreed;
> Our doctors say this is no month to bleed.
>
> (ll. 153–57)

That is flighty, effete, and narcissistic, but to sneer knowingly at Richard while he speaks it is altogether pleasurable for an audience. Richard does open the play with the six-line sentence I referred to earlier:

> Old John of Gaunt, time-honored Lancaster,
> Hast thou, according to thy oath and band,
> Brought hither Henry Hereford, thy bold son,
> Here to make good the boist'rous late appeal,
> Which then our leisure would not let us hear,
> Against the Duke of Norfolk, Thomas Mowbray?
>
> (ll. 1–6)

That sentence is gratuitously stuffed, and, what is more, threatens (in "the . . . late appeal, / Which then our leisure would not let us hear") to come loose from any anchorage in specifics; but this is the start of the play, and the royal flourish of names identifies characters for us. Moreover, in this scene Bolingbroke and Mowbray speak more than Richard and are more eager than Richard is to hobble and freight their sentences. The sentences in scene 1 testify as much as their content and lack of content to the ineffectuality of Richard's rule, but, although the *scene* is theatrically frustrating, Richard himself is not.

What I have said about syntax can seem the logical prologue to an indictment of all periodic sentences and all verbal pageantry. But, of course, it is not. There is a difference between these periodic sentences and ones in which intervening modifiers actually and pertinently modify the syntactical essentials. There is also a difference between the effect of bombast inside a periodic sentence and bombast that trails off the end of a simple clause. Bombast in a periodic sentence doubles in effectual volume. As to verbal pageantry, I would make a distinction between the vagrant formalities of scene 1 and the chivalric foreplay of marshal, combatants, and heralds in scene 3. There the language billows, but billows like a flag, and serves the same theatrically pleasurable function as the ceremonial reenactment of the coin toss before a football game.

In fact, scene 3 is as smooth and titillating as silk until Richard throws down his warder. From the moment he does that, Richard also becomes verbally frustrating. Holinshed says that Bolingbroke and Mowbray had to wait two hours to hear Richard's decree. Shakespeare allows only the length of a trumpet flourish, but he retains the effect of a two-hour wait by substituting for it syntactically. After Richard says "Draw near, / And list what with our council we have done" (1.3.123–24), he takes fifteen lines to reach his decree. He begins with two lines of anticipatory modification:

> For that our kingdom's earth should not be soiled
> With that dear blood which it hath fostered:
> (ll. 125–26)

Ready now to come to the point, he offers two more lines of modification, effectively apposite to the first two:

> And for our eyes do hate the dire aspect
> Of civil wounds ploughed up with neighbors' sword;
> (ll. 127–28)

He then sets forward on another addition, but this "And for" unit spreads hugely and accentuates its superfluity in its own formal terms—the formal terms established by the pattern of two-line units—by delaying the promised assertion for ten lines instead of two:

> And for we think the eagle-wingèd pride
> Of sky-aspiring and ambitious thoughts
> With rival-hating envy set on you
> To wake our peace, which in our country's cradle
> Draws the sweet infant breath of gentle sleep;
> Which so roused up with boist'rous untuned drums,

> With harsh-resounding trumpets' dreadful bray
> And grating shock of wrathful iron arms,
> Might from our quiet confines fright fair peace,
> And make us wade even in our kinred's blood.
> (ll. 129–38)

Only then, fifteen lines from his promise, does he deliver the verdict: "Therefore we banish you our territories."

Delay is not Richard's only resource for frustrating comprehension. This speech forces one's understanding through a series of miniscule contortions on its way to the obvious. Look at the words immediately preceding and immediately following the consultative trumpet flourish. In line 121 "Withdraw with us" is—as is immediately obvious on the stage—addressed to the council, and "Draw near," two lines later, is addressed to Bolingbroke and Mowbray. However, one hears an orderly parallel that is only verbally neat.

Something similar occurs in the lines that frame the trumpet flourish: "While we return these dukes what we decree" (l. 122) and, after the flourish, "And list what with our council we have done" (l. 124). The meaning *while* has in "while we return these dukes" gives twentieth-century readers some trouble; it means "until." Moreover, *while* would here have given Shakespeare's audience some momentary trouble too; *while* meaning "until" was already rare, and in this speech that meaning is dictated only after the fact by the verb *return*; the logical necessities of the preceding construction ("withdraw . . . and let the trumpets sound") prepare an audience to hear the word *while* in its standard sense, "in the time during which": "let the trumpets sound while."

When the conference is over, Richard calls the combatants to him so that he may "report what we decree," and, in his slow fashion, that is what he does. "We banish you our territories" (l. 139) fits the syntactic promise of line 122; but it does not fit the syntactic promise of line 124: "List what with our council we have done."

Also note the formal orderliness and syntactical mushiness of the chiasmic pairs "wake . . . which" in line 132 and "which . . . roused up" in line 134; the antecedent for the first *which* is the obvious one—the preceding word, *peace*: "peace, which in our country's cradle"; the antecedent for the second *which*, the one in "which so roused up with boist'rous untuned drums," would probably turn out to have been *pride* (l. 129), *thoughts* (l. 130), or *envy* (l. 131)—would turn out so if a listener ever could, or ever cared to, figure it out. The significance of *which* wanders idly as we listen: *sleep* is the syntactically obvious candidate, but *sleep* cannot be *roused up*; *peace*, therefore, becomes antecedent for this *which* as for the preceding one ("peace so roused up with—peace so roused up *by*—boist'rous untuned drums"); however, by the time the clause gets to a verb and object three lines later, *peace* has become the rouser of *peace* and, in transit, the *with* that meant "by"—indicated the rousing agents (*drums, trumpets' bray, grating shock)*—as we heard it in line 134 and again in line 135 has come to be as it would have been if it had been understood as "by means of"—indicating the means (*drums, trumpets' bray, grating shock*) used by the rousing agent (the subject of *Might . . . fright* in line 137): "might with drums . . . trumpets' bray . . . and grating shock . . . fright fair peace from our confines."

That sort of syntactic palimpsest is the stuff of Shakespeare's grandest, most typically Shakespearean effects: a description of the vagueness of *with* and *which* in this clause of Richard's follows the same pattern as potential descriptions of passages in—say—*Twelfth Night* or *Macbeth* where by constructive vagueness Shakespeare gives metaphysically physical location to airy nothings—lets us understand more than reason says we can. The difference is that here the extra understanding is—like the whole clause—*only* extra. The clause takes its listener meandering through ideational territory already encompassed by the simple construction signaled at the start. The waste and chaos of civil war is less impressive than the wastefulness and chaos of Richard's sentence.

The long sentence that finally arrives at "we banish you" has formal solidity—in the sound of *for* (first meaning "so that" in line 125, then meaning "because" in lines 127 and 129, and finally in the second syllable of *therefore* in line 139), but the form, like the first fifteen lines of the speech, is its own excuse—the framework for an empty house of words.

Richard, who in line 149 says he pronounces Mowbray's doom with some unwillingness, pronounces everything so. He is willing to talk and talk, to pronounce sentences, but unwilling to pronounce any *sentence*—to say out what he wants said. The speech in which Richard banishes Mowbray is an emblem of that unwillingness: the first clause is promissory, and the substance of the speech follows slowly, stuffed out with lines that assert endless tedium and imitate it. When Richard finally pronounces Mowbray's doom, he does so in an inverted, logically tortuous clause that focuses on itself and on Richard as speaker rather than on Mowbray as hearer:

> Norfolk, for thee remains a heavier doom,
> Which I with some unwillingness pronounce:
> The sly slow hours shall not determinate
> The dateless limit of thy dear exile.
> The hopeless word of "never to return"
> Breathe I against thee, upon pain of life.
> (ll. 148–53)

Once again Richard's action—a speech act—"I banish you forever"—is clear and obvious but not quite made; what one hears is distant by an easy but gratuitous leap from what one understands.

Richard's frustration of action and frustrating language, presented sequentially when he drops the warder and then announces his decision, is echoed a few lines later when he recalls the departing Mowbray:

> Return again and take an oath with thee.
> Lay on our royal sword your banished hands;
> Swear by the duty that you owe to God
> (Our part therein we banish with yourselves)
> To keep the oath that we administer;
> You never shall, so help you truth and God,
> Embrace each other's love in banishment;
> Nor never look upon each other's face;
> Nor never write, regreet, nor reconcile
> This low'ring tempest of your home-bred hate;
> Nor never by advisèd purpose meet
> To plot, contrive, or complot any ill
> 'Gainst us, our state, our subjects, or our land.
> (ll. 178–90)

Where earlier he frustrated the physical completion of the scene first and then complemented that action verbally in the syntax of his decree—physical, visible indecisiveness and verbal counterproductivity are here simultaneous. Mowbray has started to leave the stage. His part in the scene is over. Richard then calls him back; Richard thus does to the scene something like what he does to his sentences. Moreover, Richard causes Mowbray and Bolingbroke to present an onstage tableau of precisely the action they swear never to take: they join their hands and swear together; in fact, they even cooperate—like Rosencrantz and Guildenstern—in a shared sentence:

> BOLINGBROKE: I swear.
> MOWBRAY: And I, to keep all this,
> (ll. 191–92)

The syntax of the speech that promotes the cooperative response also enacts the fusion it prohibits. The first line pertains only to Mowbray (only he is in the act of departing, and *thee* is singular): "Return again and take an oath with thee." The rest of the speech is addressed to Mowbray and Bolingbroke jointly.

Richard's speech beginning "Return again" multiplies itself in a self-indulgent series of fragments governed by *nor* (much as the decree speech did in *for*). Its opening phrase both echoes and contradicts Richard's own "hopeless word of 'never to return.' " The next clause, "take an oath with thee," is superfluously complicated by first presenting the appropriate idiom "take an oath" (Richard does want Mowbray to take an oath), and then presenting "take an oath with" (Richard does want Mowbray to swear jointly with Bolingbroke), and then by erasing both in the frivolous literalization of *take* that is dictated by *thee*, the last word of the clause: "carry an oath along with thee." Three lines later, in line 181, Richard interrupts the already stuffed "swear by God to" construction with the vaingloriously magnanimous parenthesis, "Our part therein we banish with yourselves," a parenthesis so thoughtless and so casually self-serving that Richard just as casually revokes it in the last three lines of the speech.

The rhetorical efficiency of this paper would be considerably enhanced if Richard's syntax were consistently perverse from scene 3 until his departure for Ireland. Unfortunately, however, Shakespeare's practice is never as neat as a satisfying critical analysis would have it be. In fact, once Richard has denied finality to a decisive gesture one more time—by reopening the closed issue of Bolingbroke's term of banishment and—with minimal public-relations benefit to himself—reducing it, both his syntax and his assertions became notably crisp and straightforward in both manner and matter. For instance, his last lines in scene 3 are "Cousin, farewell; and, uncle, bid him so. / Six years we banish him, and he shall go." In fact, cold, foolhardy, curtness briefly becomes Richard's verbal hallmark in the scene at Gaunt's deathbed, Richard's last scene before leaving the stage for a full act, the last scene in which he has the demi-god's power he assumes he has.

But it is the ineffectual Richard I am concerned with here—not the Richard who efficiently misuses his power, but the Richard who has power and wastes it. The ineffectual Richard is in spectacular evidence in act 1, scene 4, the private scene between Richard and his cronies, the scene in which he is called to Gaunt's bedside. There Richard's syntax is as effete as he is. His sentences take every means to minimize the authority of their grammatical subjects over their verbs. Richard's sentences are passive or passive in effect, and their subjects are likely to be indefinite (as in " 'tis doubt, / When time shall call him home from banishment, / Whether . . ." [1.4.20–22]). Consider lines 59 and 60 of act 1, scene 4. Even when Richard wants to speak callously about Gaunt, he removes himself from the action of his sentence five different ways so that the immediacy of his concluding word, *immediately,* is entirely dissipated: "Now put it, God, in the physician's mind / To help him to his grave immediately"—a syntactically perverse imperative directed to the deity to put the anticipatory object (*it*) in the mind of a third being to take a minimally forceful action (*help*).

Above all, Richard does everything he can to separate any grammatical subject from its verb. For instance, in line 42, "We will ourself in person to this war," Richard is himself the grammatical subject, but he uses the royal *we*, says *we will,* interrupts the construction with *ourself* and *in person*, and then arrives at the main verb, "go," which is only elliptically present. This general tendency reaches its extreme in lines 23 and 24, which seem to have baffled the printers and have come down to us in their apparently authoritative state only in the sixth quarto: "Ourself and Bushy, Bagot here, and Green / Observed."

In the next scene Richard leaves for Ireland, and we never see a callously efficient, executive Richard again. Richard does not return at all until act 3, scene 2, by which time he has become the political underdog, a victim—albeit a guilty victim. From that point until the last seconds of his life (when he kills two of his murderers), Richard is gloriously, self-indulgently, volubly, extravagantly, ineffectual. When Richard returns in act 3, scene 2, his circumstances have altered violently, but his personality has not changed at all. And yet, as many commentators have noticed, audiences now like him better; we recognize him as the contemptible human being he always was, but we no longer find him "hard to take." Common sense rightly says that we like Richard in decline and defeat because he is the underdog, but in

Macbeth much more sympathetic circumstances have done nothing to make audiences warm to Malcolm.

One thing about Richard has changed: his syntax. He opens with an inverted—but not complex—question ("Barkloughly Castle call they this at hand?"), and his answer to Aumerle's succeeding question to him is, though another inversion, a stock idiomatic one ("Needs must I like it well"). But from there on, although Richard's imagination is flighty and extravagant, the syntax of the speech is down to earth; in fact, as he speaks he gets down to earth literally—he gets down and touches the ground:

> Needs must I like it well. I weep for joy
> To stand upon my kingdom once again.
> Dear earth, I do salute thee with my hand,
> Though rebels wound thee with their horses' hoofs.
> As a long-parted mother with her child
> Plays fondly with her tears and smiles in meeting,
> So weeping, smiling, greet I thee, my earth,
> And do thee favors with my royal hands.
> Feed not thy sovereign's foe, my gentle earth,
> Nor with thy sweets comfort his ravenous sense;
> But let thy spiders that suck up thy venom,
> And heavy-gaited toads, lie in their way,
> Doing annoyance to the treacherous feet
> Which with usurping steps do trample thee.
> Yield stinging nettles to mine enemies;
> And when they from thy bosom pluck a flower,
> Guard it, I pray thee, with a lurking adder
> Whose double tongue may with a mortal touch
> Throw death upon thy sovereign's enemies.
> Mock not my senseless conjuration, lords.
> This earth shall have a feeling, and these stones
> Prove armèd soldiers ere her native king
> Shall falter under foul rebellion's arms.
>
> (3.2.4–26)

Some of the furniture of this speech—earth, its wounds, babies—is the furniture of the tortuous speech that dragged its ornamental way from "list what with our council we have done" to "Therefore we banish you," but each clause of this speech gets to its syntactic point quickly: "I weep for joy," "I do salute thee," "Feed not thy sovereign's foe," and so on. Moreover, in these sentences subject and verb are generally right next to each other; even "greet I thee," though inverted, brings verb, subject, and object into immediate contact with one another. From this speech until the end of the play, Richard makes one lengthy, extravagant, self-indulgent speech after another, but, with very few exceptions, he makes them in straightforward syntax. His conjurations tend still to be senseless, but they make what sense they have *for* us. Richard still goes on futile, periphrastic, metaphoric, hyperbolic journeys, but his sentences now march, one step after another; and our minds do not have to dodge back and forth across the surface of his sentences or make bridges between the syntax of one speech and the imperfectly matched syntax of a response to it. From the time Richard returns from Ireland, his sentences *deliver*; they deliver the same old stuff, but they bring it right up to the door of understanding.

Having now argued the limited thesis set forth in my first paragraph, I should insist on its limitations. Habitual readers of literary criticism may well fear that, in presenting syntax as *a* cause of our negative responses to Richard in the first two acts and our positive response to him in the last three, I am presenting syntax as *the* cause—as an alternative to the major and obvious sources of those responses: the situations and events of the story. In suggesting that syntactical structures have rhetorical power, I do not mean to suggest any power for them that is not auxiliary to, and dependent on, substantial factors. I should also disclaim any implication that the particular stylistic phenomenon I have discussed always has the same rhetorical effect. I do not at all mean to imply that the kind of syntax I have called frustrated is always frustrating to listen to or that Shakespeare reserves it to characters who repel us in the scenes where they use it. Implying that would be comparable to implying that, since the hissing of multiple *s* sounds in particular descriptions of snakes can suggest snakiness, multiple *s* sounds have that metaphoric capacity inherently and in all contexts.

In the case of *Richard II* the disclaimer is urgent because there is an inadequate but tempting abundance of evidence to suggest that Shakespeare uses self-delaying syntaxes to the same rhetorical effect throughout the play. For instance, the brutally efficient Northumberland can be brutally inefficient syntactically (e.g., 3.3.105–12, where six lines of idle and idly proliferating modification separate the main verb, "swears," and its object, "[that] his coming hither"). Similarly, Bolingbroke—whose chief rhetorical asset in his relations with the audience during the last two acts of the play is his relative taciturnity in a sea of words—engages in gratuitous syntactic delays—pads out the spaces between noun, verb, and object—in act 3, scene 1, the point in the play when audience esteem for him is, for other reasons, at its lowest ebb: in his most recent previous appearance on stage Bolingbroke had substituted wordplay for logic in justifying his illegal return from France on the implied grounds that Hereford was banished but Lancaster was not (2.3.113–14); now, in cataloguing the crimes of Bushy and Bagot (who respond with unexpected spiritual nobility), Bolingbroke speaks a thirty-line speech in which the interactions of his nouns and verbs are elaborately dissipated by intervening gestures of modification; this is one example:

> Myself—a prince by fortune of my birth,
> Near to the king in blood, and near in love
> Till you did make him misinterpret me—
> Have stooped my neck under your injuries.
> (3.1.16–19)

However, although Shakespeare's use of interrupted syntax is consistently efficient and often seems rhetorically purposeful, its particular rhetorical effects vary greatly. For example, 5.2.23–28, York's lines quoted at the beginning of this essay, demonstrate just that sort of syntax, and our responses to York are very different from our responses to Northumberland in act 3, scene 3, Bolingbroke in act 3, scene 1, or Richard in acts 1 and 2. In fact, between scene 1 and Bolingbroke's invasion, the only syntax that rivals Richard's in its self-indulgence and contrived delay of predication is Gaunt's in his famous speech on Richard's future, England's past, and England's present (2.1.31–68). At the center of that speech is a twenty-one line clause in which the grammatical subject, "This royal throne of kings," and the verb, "Is now leased out," are twenty lines apart. Between them lie sixteen alternate epithets apposite to "This royal throne of kings." The epithets—each of which also begins with "this"—are intricately, but randomly and luxuriously, related (e.g., "This royal throne of kings" is echoed by "scept'red" in "this scept'red isle" and "majesty" in "This earth of majesty," while "throne" is echoed in "seat" in the third apposite phrase, "this seat of Mars"); the interchangeability of the epithets, insistently marked by the repeating *this*, is balanced by complicating variations (such as the epithet "demi-paradise" [l. 42], which, lacking the introductory *this,* and specifically relevant to the specific epithet it succeeds, acts primarily as an apposite epithet *to* an apposite epithet, "This other Eden," and also, but secondarily, as still another independent apposite to "This royal throne of kings")—and also by erratic variations in volume (the fifth epithet, "This fortress" [l. 43], has a line and a half of modification; the eighth, "This precious stone" [l. 46], has another line and a half ["set in the silver sea, / Which serves it in the office of a wall"] and then two more lines of alternate modification ["Or as a moat"]; the fourteenth, "this teeming womb of royal kings" [l. 51] leads into a wandering five-line appendage in which "kings" is modified first by the potentially ironic phrase "Feared by their breed" and its complexly related and more straightforwardly wholesome twin "and famous by their birth," and then by the still more complexly related and still more straightforward "Renownèd for their deeds," which phrase is in turn modified by "as far from home . . . / As is the sepulchre . . ." [an interrupting phrase that is itself interrupted by the syntactically redundant "For Christian service and true chivalry"]; the sepulchre is then placed geographically: "in stubborn Jewry"—a phrase in which "stubborn" is a gratuitously informative and gratuitously multivalent element in a particularly arch periphrasis).

When finally he puts a predicate to his subject, Gaunt inserts a parenthetical comment on his achievement: "I die pronouncing it"; but he thereupon stretches the clause and his faculties further by adding a simile ("Like to a tenement") and then a superfluous alternative to it ("or pelting farm"). Finished at last, Gaunt starts again, presenting two apposite echoes of the whole of the long apposite-swollen preceding clause:

> Is now leased out (I die pronouncing it)
> Like to a tenement or pelting farm.
> England, bound in with the triumphant sea,
> Whose rocky shore beats back the envious siege
> Of wat'ry Neptune, is now bound in with shame,
> With inky blots and rotten parchment bonds.
> That England that was wont to conquer others
> Hath made a shameful conquest of itself.
>
> (ll. 59–66)

Whatever other function Gaunt's syntax may have in act 2, scene 1, it is—as the parenthesis in line 59 overtly testifies—a self-fulfilling stage direction: Gaunt's syntax tells the actor to gasp and strain to get his words out, and it also makes it hard for the actor to do otherwise. Although Gaunt's self-indulgent syntax is very like the syntax Richard uses in the preceding scenes, the effects are not. The substance of Gaunt's speech and the situation in which he speaks are—as common sense knows—the principal determiners of audience response to him, just as the same factors are the vital determiners of our responses to Richard. Careful critical examination of the substance of Gaunt's speech will reveal repellent qualities in it. However, modern audiences have found Gaunt a wholly sympathetic character, and his aria on England—far from irritating audiences—has thrilled them; moreover, since an excerpt from the speech was anthologized under the heading "Albion" in *England's Parnassus* in 1600, there is reason to think that Shakespeare's audiences responded as modern ones do.

In act 2, scene 1, the dying Gaunt adopts not only Richard's previous syntactic habits but his willingness to use plays on words as valid evidence in articulating his arguments (e.g., "inspired" [l. 31] and "expiring" [l. 32] in response to York's " 'Tis breath thou lack'st, and that breath wilt thou lose"; and the play between "leased *out*" [l. 59] and "bound *in*" [ll. 61, 63] and the play between the two uses of "bound in"; in Gaunt's first speech after Richard arrives to visit him, he plays "so nicely" on his name that Richard himself wonders at it [l. 84]).

I cannot imagine that any audience was ever conscious of the syntactical likeness between Gaunt's last speeches and Richard's in the earlier scenes. Nor do I posit audiences conscious that Gaunt's wordplay in act 2, scene 1, is Richard-like. However, Shakespeare seems very much concerned to establish a parallel between the physically doomed Gaunt and the politically doomed Richard. Gaunt asserts the likeness overtly in a long speech (ll. 93–115) that begins thus:

> Now, he that made me knows I see thee ill;
> Ill in myself to see, and in thee seeing ill.
> Thy deathbed is no lesser than thy land,
> Wherein thou liest in reputation sick.

At the end of the speech Shakespeare dramatizes, and thus reinforces, the equation of Gaunt and Richard with a syntactic trick. As Gaunt seems about to conclude his tirade, Richard interrupts him with an abusive epithet. Both the succeeding syntax and the probabilities of the situation indicate that the epithet is vocative and describes Gaunt; so does its inclusion of "lean-witted," which is yet another play on

Gaunt's name; but the epithet also completes both the syntax and the line of thought it interrupts:

> GAUNT: Landlord of England art thou now, not king.
> Thy state of law is bondslave to the law,
> And thou—
> RICHARD: A lunatic lean-witted fool.

Close examination suggests (1) that Shakespeare purposefully set about showing us a likeness between Richard and Gaunt in act 2, scene 1, and (2) that Shakespeare was there conscious of syntax as a rhetorical tool. (The artful interrelation of a discussion [ll. 1–30] and a demonstration [ll. 31–68] of the paradox of Gaunt's verbosity and his shortness of breath suggests that Shakespeare was purposeful in choosing and manipulating syntactic structures for rhetorical ends; so does the ironic coherence of Gaunt's interrupted sentence and the epithet with which Richard breaks it off in line 115.) Close examination of act 2, scene 1, thus also suggests that Shakespeare might have designed Gaunt's Richard-like syntax in the "England" speech to prepare the way for the overt parallel to follow. There is, however, no way to measure the extent to which Gaunt's speech patterns color or inform an audience's subconscious; moreover, whatever his success, Shakespeare's intentions are a matter of concern to students of Shakespeare rather than students of the play.

On the other hand, the frustrated syntax of the frustrated Gaunt of act 2, scene 1, participates in one of the largest and most universally remarked characteristics of the play: its tendency to evoke contempt for words (as opposed to physical facts). I suggest that simple wordiness, talking a lot, is a consistent and rhetorically efficient metaphor for any and all varieties of weakness in *Richard II*—sometimes one or another kind of spiritual insufficiency (Bolingbroke in 3.1, Northumberland in 3.3, Richard throughout), sometimes one or another kind of physical insufficiency (Carlisle in 4.1, York and both duchesses throughout, Gaunt in 2.1). I suggest that frustrated syntaxes like Richard's at the beginning of the play and Gaunt's at his death make wordiness feel extreme and suggestive of extreme weakness. Most importantly, I suggest that Shakespeare's failure to discriminate consistently between the speech patterns of morally weak speakers and physically weak ones—or between weak characters we like and weak characters we dislike—or between the strong, silent, admirable Gaunt of act 1, scene 1, and the strong, silent, monstrous Northumberland of act 5, scene

1—is of the essence of this play, is an auxiliary factor in generating the subtly pervasive moral uneasiness audiences and critics feel about themselves as they think back on the way their minds have behaved during *Richard II*—a play in which one is often at the point of catching one's mind in the act of forgetting that might is not right.

By way of token illustration of what I said about the general rhetorical functions of reticence and verbosity in *Richard II*, I will conclude by giving an account of Gaunt's verbal career similar to the one I earlier gave of Richard's.

Richard and Gaunt are compared and contrasted from the first moments of the play, and the point of comparison is the verbal characteristics of the two. The visual inevitabilities of the entrance of king and court focus an audience's attention on Richard, and that focus is confirmed when he is the first to speak; but the first words he speaks, the first words of the play, are "Old John of Gaunt, time-honored Lancaster." The six lines of iambic pentameter in which Richard embeds the question "Hast thou brought hither Henry Hereford" draw four syllables of crisp prose from Gaunt: "I have my liege." The contrast between Richard and Gaunt is similarly played out in the next two speeches. Richard asks another inflated question in regular verse. Gaunt's answer is three lines long—almost as long as Richard's question—but it is constructed so as to sound curtly utilitarian; the first line is prose and is a syntactic fragment dependent on Richard's question for its implied syntax; the last phrase, "no inveterate malice" is only elliptically connected to the sentence it so briskly concludes:

> KING: Tell me, moreover, hast thou sounded him
> If he appeal the duke on ancient malice,
> Or worthily, as a good subject should,
> On some known ground of treachery in him?
> GAUNT: As near as I could sift him on that argument,
> On some apparent danger seen in him
> Aimed at your highness, no inveterate malice.
> (ll. 8–14)

That three-line answer is the longest speech Gaunt makes in scene 1; moreover, although he strikes an audience as a strong fourth among the parties to the scene, Gaunt has only two more speeches in scene 1—for a total of four (the others are rhymed couplets [ll. 160–61, 162–63] in which Gaunt and Richard cooperate in attempting to calm

Bolingbroke and Mowbray). In terms of the working distinction I outlined earlier, Gaunt is the "best character" in scene 1, a scene so freighted with inefficient, inconclusive, syntactically swollen verbal posturing that reticence is the most winning quality a character can have.

The next scene is Gaunt's conversation with the Duchess of Gloucester. Gaunt has more to say (seventeen lines), but the Duchess has two lines for every one of his. Moreover, Gaunt's syntax is again abbreviated, and Shakespeare again takes pains to make his audience feel the superfluity of what is said by a speaker other than Gaunt. Just over half-way through scene 2 the Duchess declares the scene over: "Farewell, old Gaunt" (l. 44); thereupon she goes on for eleven more lines, concluding with another farewell—this one extra final because it is in a rhymed couplet; Gaunt answers with a farewell couplet of his own:

> DUCHESS: Farewell, old Gaunt. Thy sometimes brother's wife
> With her companion, Grief, must end her life.
> GAUNT: Sister, farewell; I must to Coventry.
> As much good stay with thee as go with me!
> (ll. 54–57)

Those lines, just over two-thirds of the way through act 1, scene 2, are Gaunt's last in the scene. The Duchess thereupon continues the scene for another seventeen lines (ll. 58–74), lines which not only feel formally superfluous but include explicit reference to the inconclusiveness of formal conclusions:

> Yet one word more! Grief boundeth where it falls
> Not with the empty hollowness, but weight.
> I take my leave before I have begun,
> For sorrow ends not when it seemeth done.
> (ll. 58–61)

In scene 3 Gaunt enters with Richard at line 6, but, up to the point where Richard cancels the duel and banishes the combatants, Gaunt speaks only once (1.3.78–83). As compared with his previous linguistic behavior that six-line exhortation of his son is luxurious, but the speech is efficient and crisp in effect. After the sentencing, Mowbray's departure, and Richard's reduction of Bolingbroke's term of banishment, Gaunt's syntax remains straightforward, but, in his frustration, he becomes very talkative. Gaunt speaks more than half of the last hundred lines of scene 3. Moreover, his suggestion that Bolingbroke change his condition by reimagining it (ll. 275–93) is Richard-like in its substance. In Gaunt's next scene, his last, he is dying—physically impotent. There he speaks the huge, syntactically protracted, hugely paraphrastic "England" speech; and there, for the first time, he begins to behave as if he mistook the manipulation of words for the manipulation of things.

Richard II to *Henry IV*: Variations on the Fall

James L. Calderwood

As the deposed Richard II sits alone at Pomfret Castle musing on his losses, his only apparent consolation is an abundance of metaphors bestowed upon him by a generous playwright. The most extravagant of these is his sustained conceit identifying himself as Time's "numbering clock":

> I wasted time, and now doth Time waste me,
> For now hath Time made me his numbering clock.
> My thoughts are minutes, and with sighs they jar
> Their watches on unto mine eyes, the outward watch,
> Whereto my finger, like a dial's point,
> Is pointing still, in cleansing them from tears.
> Now sir, the sound that tells what hour it is
> Are clamorous groans, which strike upon my heart,
> Which is the bell. So sighs and tears and groans
> Show minutes, times, and hours. But my time
> Runs posting on in Bolingbroke's proud joy
> While I stand fooling here, his Jack o' the clock.
>
> (5.5.49–60)

The ironies of the time-waster now wasted by time, though they eloquently express the pathos of Richard's plight, seem a small semantic return on a poetic investment of twelve lines. However, if the

---

From *Metadrama in Shakespeare's Henriad*. © 1979 by the Regents of the University of California. University of California Press, 1979.

plight of the unemployed sovereign in prison figures that of *his* sovereign, the poet-playwright Shakespeare, then at that level of interpretation this clock may tell us more than timely truths.

In the first place, as "teller" (l. 55), that is, as true reflector or measuring device, the clock as such is notoriously prone to error, especially in an England that had yet to establish Greenwich as a final temporal authority (even though another great temporal authority, Elizabeth, was born there). In the second place, though Shakespeare probably considered time as part of the natural cosmic order, he could hardly help knowing that of all temporal units the "minutes, times, and hours" he emphasizes here are the most arbitrary—since days, months, seasons, and years are at least based on periodicity in nature. This stress upon the arbitrary and distorting features of temporal representation is reinforced by the fact that Richard's bodily clock reflects his internal state, so that the external representation of time (the "outward watch" of eyes, finger, heart) is governed by the subjective experience of time. The overall effect of the conceit is to bring home to us the extent to which time is humanly created rather than mimetically measured, and hence how fundamentally cut off from time man is. The temporal *Ding an sich* is presumably out there somewhere, but it is available to man only through the deflecting prism of his symbolic representations. The clock thus asserts the disjunction of man and nature (time) at the very moment that it serves imperfectly to unite the two.

The wayward artificiality of the clock as a teller of nature's truths is mirrored verbally by the strained, rhetorical self-consciousness (for example, "Now sir") of Richard's conceit telling of the clock. All of Richard's metaphors during the latter part of the play and especially at Pomfret Castle exhibit this air of uneasy contrivance. As metaphors they appear to assert an equation of tenor and vehicle—usually of Richard and the world outside his prison—much as the clock presents itself as a true teller of time. But they are metaphors in which Richard no longer believes, and which therefore imply a chasm between him and the world in the very attempt to bridge it:

> I have been studying how I may compare
> This prison where I live unto the world.
> And for because the world is populous
> And here is not a creature but myself,
> I cannot do it. *Yet I'll hammer it out.*

> My brain I'll prove the female to my soul,
> My soul the father, and these two beget
> A generation of *still-breeding thoughts,*
> And these same thoughts people this little world
> In humours *like* the people of this world.
> (5.5.1–10; my italics)

What Richard hammers out as a labor of will rather than of belief is a series of metaphoric likenesses whose ambiguous success in connecting him to the world outside is indicated by the fact that they will prove "still-breeding"—ever-and-never-breeding at once, always-bearing and yet stillborn. Ultimately, however, Richard's thoughts can populate only "this little world," the nursery of his own mind, unable to pass beyond likeness and become authentic citizens in the larger world outside. Metaphors, after all, are not the thing itself.

Symbols had not always seemed so isolated from reality. Indeed, on Richard's unexamined assumptions, language had been bonded to nature and the world order by virtue of God's certification of him as a Divine Right king. The original power of the divine Word remained actively at work in the King's English, just as divine authority descending by way of primogeniture was immanent in Richard himself. But it is the purpose of the play to divest Richard of these views—to drive a wedge between words and their meanings, between the world order and the word order, between the king and the man who is king, and between names and metaphors. Thus we find in *Richard II* not merely the fall of a king but also the fall of kingly speech—of a speech conceived of as sacramental and ontological, in which words are not proxies for things but part of the things themselves. With the fall of this King's English there falls also a view of reality contained within it, a view so similar to the "world picture" attributed to Elizabeth's reign that the parallels might well seem vexing to anyone who worked in words. "I am Richard II," Elizabeth told William Lombarde, "Know ye not that?" In 1595 Elizabeth had not yet played Richard II to Essex's Bolingbroke, but her language—the English on which playwrights like Shakespeare drew—was already beginning to play Richard II to Sir Francis Bacon's Bolingbroke. [Elsewhere,] I have outlined this general shift from verbal fideism to skepticism during the sixteenth and seventeenth centuries. Shakespeare, however, comes at these matters dramatically. Like Richard in Pomfret Castle, he addresses himself not to linguistic theory, but to homelier things like names and metaphors.

Losing his name, Richard loses everything. Cast out of his medieval world of preestablished order and significance, he is isolated in Pomfret Castle where he attempts, with stiff rhetorical flourishes, to hammer out meanings that had once simply been there for his taking. His resort to metaphor is inevitable once the old names are gone, for metaphor is the language of the unnamed. The process is familiar. Lacking a vocabulary for the unnamed, we steal from the already named. Each successful new metaphor is a creative insight and for a time gives off a spark of aesthetic pleasure. So long as tension exists between tenor and vehicle—so long as there is an element of the negative in our awareness that it is not what it literally claims to be—the metaphor remains metaphoric. With wear, however, this tension slackens, and the metaphor collapses into an inert name—or more familiarly "dies." Thus few people today hear the "call" of the word *vocation* or feel the "fusion of self and god" in *enthusiasm*. The fact that *baron* once meant roughly "blockhead" had been forgotten even by Shakespeare's time, when noble reminders still abounded. Language, in short, is a cemetery of dead metaphors, as linguists are fond of saying; or as poets like Emerson prefer, it is fossil poetry.

In a sense metaphor is an improper use of words, a violation of the linguistic system. Its depth structure is that of the proposition "A is B"—"Honey is sweet"—whether the tenor is present or only implied in the surface structure. But whereas none of the properties of sweetness is incompatible with honey, a metaphor cannot be a metaphor unless some, perhaps most, of its properties are incompatible with its subject. "For what els is your Metaphor," Puttenham asks, "but an inversion of sense by transport." For this reason a metaphor may initially look like a terminological error, a misnaming. When Mistress Quickly cries out to the street-fighting Falstaff "Ah thou honey-suckle villain!" and again "Thou art a honey-seed," we may spend some long moments puzzling over the honeylike properties of plump Jack before realizing that Mistress Quickly is playing hostess not to metaphor but to malapropism. She means, not "honey-suckle" and "honey-seed," but "homicidal" and "homicide" (*2 Henry IV,* 2.1.55, 59).

In Mistress Quickly's usage, error must be distinguished from apparent metaphor. Normally, it is the other way round: metaphor must earn its title to truth in a contest against error. Any new metaphor must be tested, must win its way to acceptance, its truth competing for favor against the odds of its own more obvious falseness. When in *1 Henry IV* Falstaff calls Mistress Quickly an otter, Hal challenges the term—"An otter, Sir John! Why an otter?"—thus forcing Falstaff to defend the truth of his metaphor: "Why, she's neither fish nor flesh; a man knows not where to have her" (3.3.142–45). Mistress Quickly bustles forth a convincing denial—"Thou or any man knows where to have me, thou knave, thou!" (3.3.147)—but the point is that the question of truth has arisen.

The question of truth is precisely what does not arise in the case of dead metaphors. Here, the vehicle is no longer an illuminating similitude but literally the name of the tenor. No one questions whether "far-seeing" is an appropriate term for the broadcasting of images by radiowaves to receivers that project them onto a picture tube. When the semantic batteries in a metaphor have gone entirely dead, as those of "television" have for most people and certainly for those to whom it is merely "TV," the metaphor ceases to be a metaphor and becomes a name. As such, it passes securely beyond challenges as to its truth, rightness, and acceptability. Had Falstaff said "Francis Bacon is a baron," Hal would no more have thought to challenge the dead metaphor—"A baron, Sir John! Why a baron?"—than he would to challenge the proper name, "Why 'Francis Bacon'?" To either question the only possible answer, even for a master of improvisation like Falstaff, would be a shrugging "That's simply the name." There is no relevance to search out, no insightful comparison or "before unapprehended relation of things." A name is a name is a name.

Now for Richard II kingship, *his* kingship, is as much beyond question as a proper name. It has the automatic warrant of Divine Right, which means not that Richard conceives of himself as the right king but that he conceives of himself simply as *the* king. For him "King" and "Richard" are not two words but one indissoluble name. The old metaphors linking kingly office and divine office are not analogical truths in Richard's imagination but anagogic ones, not metaphors but identities. The king is not *like,* he *is* the "deputy elected by the Lord," "God's substitute," "the Lord's lieutenant," and so on. And because "King" and "Richard" are one entity, Richard is all of these things—and so he must carry his title with him to the grave, all successors disallowed.

This seems to be why Shakespeare, despite having established (in act 1, scene 2 especially) Richard's criminal failures, even his murderousness, as king, then dramatizes his deposition not so much as a trial of Richard's conduct as a trial of his concept of the royal office. At issue is whether King and Richard are in fact one word and whether the metaphors so royally taken for granted are literally true. Thus Shakespeare charts Richard's dramatic experience by the coordinates of name and person, thrusting him from a belief in the monistic divinity of name—

> Arm, arm, my name! A puny subject strikes
> At thy great glory
>
> (3.2.86–87)

—to a recognition of dualistic separability—

> What must the King do now? Must he submit?
> The king shall do it. Must he be deposed?
> The King shall be contented. Must he lose
> The name of king? O' God's name, let it go!
>
> (3.3.143–46)

—to an ultimate loss of name and a consequent dissolution of personal identity and meaning—

> I have no name, no title;
> No, not that name was given me at the font,
> But 'tis usurped. Alack the heavy day,
> That I have worn so many winters out
> And know not what name to call myself!
>
> (4.1.255–59)

Ernst Cassirer remarks [in *Language and Myth*] that, among primitives, "the being and life of a person are so intimately connected with his name that, as long as the name is preserved and spoken, its bearer is still felt to be present and directly active." In Richard's case the ambiguity of the life-giving powers of the name is given full expression. Richard "lives" only so long as his name is honored; once that is gone, he becomes in his own word "nothing," even before his death at the hands of Exton. In Pomfret Castle he realizes that the name of king is merely arbitrary, that he has an identity apart from the name. Yet this knowledge, instead of sustaining him, instead of making him feel that he has lost "merely" a name and not life itself, destroys him. There are no "mere" words, it seems, only meaningful ones. Exton kills a man who is, in his namelessness, already dead.

Richard's world is dead too. It is a world conceived of in metaphors that had died into names, as Richard discovered too late. The metaphors he has taken literally were also taken literally in the sixteenth century, and implicit in them was a world view. Pattrick Cruttwell remarks:

> Shakespeare is not really a philosopher; he had no philosophy of his own. He didn't need to have one; it was given him. He had simply to describe human life as honestly, vividly, and completely as he knew, and then, through the very terms of reference by which alone he *could* describe it, a philosophy emerges.
>
> ("Physiology and Psychology in Shakespeare's Age," *Journal of the History of Ideas* 12 [Jan. 1951])

The philosophy that emerges, Cruttwell says, is the "integrated medieval view" that E. M. W. Tillyard has more famously, if somewhat metachronically, called the Elizabethan world picture. This world view, inherited from medieval culture, was intimately bound up with Elizabethan language, also inherited from medieval culture. The conception of a world essentially animistic, full of anthropomorphic life, dancing, ceremony, order, harmony—a hierarchical world of Platonic dualities and microspheres fashioned on the principles of analogy and parallelism—this world was not merely a set of theories in which men believed; it was what most of their key words implicitly *meant*. The world picture was a word picture. It was not for nothing that reality was thought to be composed of "elements" and nature conceived of as a "book."

But in Richard's dramatic experience—as in England's historical experience during the sixteenth and seventeenth centuries—the Book of Nature becomes incomprehensible. Things no longer answer to their assigned names. Once upon a time, in a fairy-tale world, "four lagging winters and four wanton springs [could be made to] end in a word, such [was] the breath of kings" (1.3.214–15). Once upon a time the king's name was twenty thousand names, and the king and God were consubstantial. That fairy-tale time had its historical counterpart in Shakespeare's England, as the fictive Richard had his real-life spokesman in, among others, William Tyndale, who said that

> he that judgeth the King judgeth God, and he that layeth hands on the King layeth hands on God, and he that resisteth the King resisteth God. . . . The King is in this world without law, and he may at his lust do right or wrong and shall give accounts but to God only.

These claims echo again and again through the Tudor homilies, especially in that "Concernyng Good Ordre and Obedience to Rulers and Magistrates" (1547) and that "Against Disobedience and Wilful Rebellion" (1574). That kingship confers quasi-divine status and inviolability upon its holder is owing in part to God's direct appointment of kings, an appointment renewed through primogeniture, and in part to God's establishment of hierarchical order throughout the universe. As the visible symbol of human order, the king mediates between "earthly men" and both God and God's grand design. If he falls, all else falls with him, as Ulysses, the domino theorist of *Troilus and Cressida,* so eloquently details it.

Bishop Carlisle, the Ulysses of *Richard II,* sounds a similar theme. Just before the deposition of Richard, when Bolingbroke says "In God's name, I'll ascend the regal throne," Carlisle cries "Marry, God forbid!" and in effect reads the Tudor homilies to him:

> shall the figure of God's majesty,
> His captain, steward, deputy elect,
> Anointed, crowned, planted many years,
> Be judged by subject and inferior breath,
> And he himself not present?
>
> (4.1.125–29)

The Earl of Northumberland applauds Carlisle's performance—"Well have you argued, sir"—but adds, "and for your pains / Of capital treason we arrest you here" (4.1.150–51). So much, it would seem, for Divine Right!

And so much, also, for a sacramental language in which words have a kind of divine, inalienable right to their referents. Unlike Richard, Bolingbroke has never subscribed to such a language. From the opening scene of the play he has regarded words as mere vocal conveniences whose substance lies not in themselves but in what they designate. Thus he employs words as promissory notes in gathering followers in his venture for kingship, and reinforces what few words he does utter with material force. At Flint Castle, where Richard descends to the base court with many words and few soldiers, Bolingbroke listens politely and says little: his twenty thousand soldiers are all the eloquence he requires. If Richard is a regal name that is gradually divested of its meaning, Bolingbroke is a kind of material force or meaning in search of the name that will give him public expression.

The name Bolingbroke seeks is, of course, "king," and the bond between word and meaning is analogous to that between kingship and the holder of that office. If the king's name or title normally goes unquestioned, it is not, Richard discovers, because it is divinely guaranteed but because it is humanly conferred and assumed. Names fit their referents not because of an underlying correspondence or substantive unity but by virtue of informal covenants among speakers. Kings and meanings rule by custom. It follows, as Bolingbroke well knows, that the name of "king" will as readily answer to the meaning of "Henry IV" as to that of "Richard II." The next step in this reduction of language from the sacrosanct to the purely arbitrary is registered by Falstaff's remark to Prince Hal at the opening of *1 Henry IV*: "I would to God thou and I knew where a commodity of good names were to be bought" (1.2.92–94). Like money, language is now reckoned a merely useful social instrument. Its meaning and value are no longer intrinsic but manufactured in response to the vicissitudes of the marketplace. In the inflationary times of *2 Henry IV* the value of the word will fall still further. But that is to get ahead of the story.

When words are divorced from things, when names are seen to have neither a magical nor an inherently natural connection to their referents, then meaning comes into question, both in language and in kingship. What, during the reign of Bolingbroke, does the name of "king" mean? *Richard II* has presented us with the gradual estrangement of the name "king" from the meaning which, in the person of Richard himself, it has expressed, a meaning underwritten by God. If the royal name still presumes to mean "the Lord's lieutenant" or "God's substitute," then the proposition "The King is Henry IV" can only be a lie, as Hotspur and the other conspirators feel. If, on the other hand, the proposition is true, if Bolingbroke *is* "King Henry IV," then the old meanings are, and must always have been, not literal but only metaphorical. If so, the king is not a participant in divinity but an actor in a secular role, as Richard appears to realize in his tiring-room at Pomfret Castle:

> Thus play I in one person many people,
> And none contented. Sometimes am I king,
> Then treasons make me wish myself a beggar,
> And so I am. Then crushing penury
> Persuades me I was better when a king;
> Then am I kinged again—and by and by

Think that I am unkinged by Bolingbroke,
And straight am nothing.

(5.5.31–38)

Richard's world of names has cracked apart to reveal the metaphor that was inert but not entirely dead within. Between "king" and such meanings as "God's substitute" stands, not an equals sign, but an "as-if." If what is true of the king's name is also true of the King's English—or, in Shakespeare's time, of the Queen's English—then the implications for the poet-playwright are inauspicious indeed.

Why, we may wonder, should Shakespeare fashion in *Richard II* not merely the fall of a king but also the fall of kingly speech? Kings have died from time to time and worms have eaten them, but not for words. Henry VI, Richard III, and John, all fall without our feeling that a world of words topples with them. Yet there is clearly a sense in which Richard's verbal experience can be seen to reflect issues of paramount interest to the poet-playwright. Indeed, Richard has often been called a poet-king, not because he speaks excellent verse—as the "unpoetic" Bolingbroke does also—but because his attitude toward language is poetic. After his return from Ireland, he ignores his captains' calls to action, preferring instead to "sit upon the ground / And tell sad stories of the deaths of kings" (3.3.155–56). That is, rather than enter on actions that would assert his authority in England, Richard lapses into forms of lyric narcissism. These sentimental verbal kingdoms are gratifying to him because within their imagined borders he holds uncontested sway; no Bolingbroke may enter there.

It is not quite accurate, however, to say that the poetic Richard whiles away his time with symbols and ceremonies at the expense of reality and action, which fall under the aegis of Bolingbroke, because in Richard's view language participates in reality, and words constitute actions. Yet Richard's journey through the play from Windsor Castle to Pomfret Castle, from Highness to nothingness, dramatizes the breakdown of this conception of symbolism and language. He experiences in miniature the whole cultural metamorphosis of language, the long historical process in which the marriage of word and thing, signifier and signified, was put asunder and man's thought divorced from his world. For Bacon, Hobbes, the Royal Society, and modern linguists, this process is a melioristic one—not a breakdown of the union between word and thing but a liberation of the word from the thing. For the poet, however, such a process is analogous to the Fall—or, in

Richard II, to the deposition of a Divine Right king. For if language even in its post-Edenic, fallen form were sacramental—if its words either contained divinity, as in the figure of Christ the Logos, or even represented divinity, as in the figure of the Divine Right monarch—then the man who held dominion over language—whether king, priest, magician, or poet—would in some degree hold dominion over things and men's minds as well. Merely by practicing his craft the poet would participate in the divine order, bringing the Book of Art into direct alignment with the Book of Nature, and acquiring by virtue of his mastery of words something of the creative authority deeply embedded in them from the beginning. He would then rebut the philistine claim that poetry is a pleasant lie, not by saying with Sidney that the poet nothing affirmeth and hence cannot lie, but by saying that his loving attendance upon language affirms a divine order and truth already implicit in words.

But for poet as well as king, it is not so. In *Richard II* Shakespeare dramatizes his awareness that his verbal medium is founded not on names but on metaphor. More precisely, within a language of names, seemingly bonded to Elizabethan reality and warranted by God, lies the altogether human presence of metaphor, its once creative energy long since hardened into conventional definition. This descent from names to metaphors implies a fall from truth also. For it is the nature of metaphor to assume the appearance of the lie, since both, as the Houyhnhnms put it, "say the thing that is not."

The linguistic issue is dramatized in terms of the royal "name." In Richard's Divine Right view, "king" is part of his own proper name—inherently legitimate, inviolable, even unquestionable. Usurped by Bolingbroke and applied to himself as "Henry IV," the name of "king" becomes ambiguous—at best, a term abruptly redefined in meaning, at worst, a lie that invades all of the King's English and breaks the bonds of meaning. What, then, of the young Prince Hal, the future king? Applied to the wastrel prince, the title of king must appear a lie too. Or, from the perspective of the tavern world, it must seem a delicious joke whose punch line will burst riotously on England shortly after Hal's coronation.

Hal is himself willing to exploit the appearance of a lie, as his first soliloquy informs us, but in the long run his view of his relation to kingship is metaphoric, and in this regard he distinguishes himself from both Richard and Bolingbroke. For him, the title will no longer possess the Divine Right status of a personal name, as it did for

Richard, because he maintains a metaphoric doubleness of focus between vehicle and tenor, name and person, never forgetting that there are ironic distinctions between His Highness Henry the Fifth and the man whom the drawers called "a Corinthian, a lad of mettle, a good boy (by the Lord, so they call me)" (*1 Henry IV,* 2.4.11–13). If the royal title is not part of his personal name, neither is it merely a piece of stolen property, like "King Henry the Fourth." As with all metaphors, Hal must somehow demonstrate the truth of his kingship in the teeth of his apparent—in fact, his heir apparent—falseness. For a Divine Right he must substitute an earned human right to the crown. Only then can kingship be invested with meaning.

And Shakespeare? He, no less than Prince Hal, is called in doubt by Bolingbroke's usurpation and the fall of speech. If the king is a lie in the political realm, the lie is now king in the verbal world—and he who practices in that world must needs seem a liar. So the would-be king Hal and the would-be playwright Shakespeare must acknowledge themselves apparent liars to begin with, and somehow wrest truth from that false appearance. Both must transcend Bolingbroke and achieve authentic sovereignty in their separate realms of politics and art.

Psychoanalyzing the Shakespeare Text: The First Three Scenes of the *Henriad*

Harry Berger, Jr.

Patriarchal ideology is shown in the *Henriad* to create deep tensions which are not dispelled, are often exacerbated, by its mechanisms of repression and displacement. This is partly because the problems inherent in the cultural constructions of "natural" or jural fatherhood are carried into the wider sphere of national and dynastic politics in two uneasily related forms of symbolic fatherhood: the Christian principle of divine paternity, and the aristocratic principle of what might be called heraldic genealogy. The name of the Father, God, is used to authorize the distribution of patriarchal power into two axes of "descent": the "vertical" axis of substitution called hierarchy, and the "horizontal" axis of succession, heraldic genealogy. In both axes, the formal "cause" or criterion is *mimesis*; but whereas, in the first, descent is organized in terms of declining resemblance to the Father, in the second, the Father ideally achieves genealogical immortality by reproducing its image in progenial replicas. My emphasis in this essay will be on a certain disorder in the mimetic principle itself, a contradiction which, as Plato saw, causes the structure of genealogical mimesis to be contaminated by that of hierarchical mimesis.

The ideal of genealogical mimesis is appealed to early in *Richard II* by the Duchess of Gloucester, who reminds Gaunt that his father's seven sons "Were as seven vials of his sacred blood, / Or seven fair branches springing from one root" (1.2.12–13), and that his murdered

---

From *Shakespeare and the Question of Theory,* edited by Patricia Parker and Geoffrey Hartman. © 1985 by Harry Berger, Jr. Methuen, 1985.

brother, her late husband, "was the model of thy father's life" (l. 28). Similarly, in 2.1, York appeals to this ideal when he urges Richard to live up to the standards set by his father, reminding him that "His face thou hast, for even so look'd he" (l. 176). A little later, he gives the principle its classic statement:

> Is not Gaunt dead? and doth not Herford live?
> Was not Gaunt just? and is not Harry true?
> Did not the one deserve to have an heir?
> Is not his heir a well-deserving son?
> Take Herford's rights away, and take from time
> His charters, and his customary rights;
> Let not to-morrow then ensue to-day:
> Be not thyself. For how art thou a king
> But by fair sequence and succession?
>
> (2.1.191–99)

Though these appear to be blandly constative articulations of the mimetic principle, they are being uttered in the face of its violation, and York's rhetoric is already charged with a sense of its fragility—a sense of the generational malaise which he will betray later in the play, and which may be imagined to motivate the blandness and the appeal of heraldic genealogy.

Consider, for example, the third and fourth lines: their chiasmic bonding does not quite efface the tension between the claims stated in the two separate rhetorical questions. Gaunt "deserves" an heir, not only because he was just, but also because he is dead. His son "deserves" to be an heir not only because he is true (we could read this mimetically as "true to his father," "in his image") but also because he is alive. The heir represents his father's death, the loss of authority, power, life—"no less than all"—and he can plead his right to this appropriation by appealing to the plague of custom and curiosity of nations.

Edmund's pungent if pathetic braveries—the clichés of knavery and folk cynicism—take on a different kind of life when transplanted to the soil of primogeniture and legitimate inheritance. For they clearly apply:

> This seems a fair deserving, and must draw me
> That which my father loses; no less than all:
> The younger rises when the old doth fall.
>
> (*King Lear,* 3.3.23–25)

York tries to secure the rhetorical icon of the transmission he is defending by the chiasmus "one—deserve—heir—heir—deserving—son": "the one" reappears at the end, but not quite, in "son"; mimesis implies and demands a difference which it tries to overcome by a mirroring that recuperates the lost identity, but the inversion that expresses the difference at the heart of the process also expresses opposition between the two orders of "the one" and "son."

The threat of external violation addressed by York in his protest to Richard thus reflects a problem lurking within the mimetic process itself, and may partially account for the ineffectuality of the protest. Such persuasions meet stiff competition in paternal criticism of sons, as exemplified by Gaunt early in *Richard II* and much later by Gaunt's son in *2 Henry IV*:

> O, had thy grandsire with a prophet's eye
> Seen how his son's son should destroy his sons,
> From forth thy reach he would have laid thy shame
>
> (*Richard II,* 2.1.104–6)

> See, sons, what things you are
>
> (*2 Henry IV,* 4.5.64)

The negative and positive sides of paternal ideology are expressed in the following two statements by Bolingbroke, the first to York, who has just disclosed his son's treason, and the second to Hal:

> O loyal father of a treacherous son!
> Thou sheer, immaculate and silver fountain,
> From whence this stream, through muddy passages,
> Hath held his current and defil'd himself,
> Thy overflow of good converts to bad
>
> (*Richard II,* 5.3.58–62)

> And now my death
> Changes the mood, for what in me was purchas'd
> Falls upon thee in a more fairer sort;
> So thou the garland wear'st successively.
>
> (*2 Henry IV,* 4.5.198–201)

But the negativity and positivity of these utterances are complicated, and indeed challenged, as soon as they are contextualized.

Psychoanalytic criticism has tended to approach the problems adumbrated by these statements by resituating them within the network of explanations made available by the institutionalized lore of psychoanalysis. I propose as an alternative taking a scion from that root and grafting it onto a different explanatory network whose stock is the mimetic process. As I mentioned earlier, there is a disorder, a structural flaw, in the very notion of mimesis, and it is magnified by confusion in the paternal deployment of the genealogical principle. The father's desire for immortality may produce a desire to clone and control an endless series of identical replacements. This, incidentally, implicates a latent ideal of male parthenogenesis which may be expressed in the fear, scapegoating, and repression of the feminine. But this desire is crossed by the desire to overgo one's replacements, to be the unrepeatable archetypical eponymous progenitor whose all-giving cannot be matched. What the father then wants to reproduce are not replicas but images, imitations. It is of the nature of an imitation to be defective, to fall short of what it represents so that it can represent itself *as* the representation of an exemplar. A perfect imitation, as Derrida notes, "is no longer an imitation"; the tiny difference between imitated and imitation makes all the difference; imitation "is not what it is . . . unless it is in some way at fault or rather in default." The paternal project entails the reduction of the son's difference, his otherness, to assure both the genealogical continuity of the paternal archetype and its hierarchic superiority to the weaker vessels that transmit its image. This is a project of symbolic filicide, and it is nourished by the desire of immortality, that is, by the fear of death which, projected onto the potential replacement, makes of a "true inheritor" a true competitor. In the space or gap of otherness which the act of paternity creates, and which symbolic filicide cannot efface, but can only render more alien, arises the answering project of symbolic parricide.

The centrality of this theme to the *Henriad* has often been recognized and discussed, but with two limitations which I shall try to confront in this essay. First, the burden of critical discussion has been placed on Henry IV as father; virtually no attention has been paid to him as son, and this will be the subject of the following interpretation. Second, I know of no serious attempts to correlate psychoanalytic criticism with the two other major lines of interpretation addressed to the *Henriad*, political and metatheatrical criticism. And while I do not have space to consider there in any detail, I shall illustrate and formulate a methodological hypothesis for connecting metatheatrical issues to the intratextual representation of political and generational conflict.

For reasons that will become clearer as we proceed, a metatheatrical approach to the dramatic and theatrical dimensions of the "story" of the *Henriad* presupposes a standpoint outside the normative limits of what has been called "stage-centered" reading. It calls for a project that is doggedly textual in orientation, and is thus *anti*theatrical: it will generate readings that do not readily lend themselves to performance and that will necessarily draw fire from stage-centered critics. But that, in a perverse way, is my point: that the antitheatricality of the readings I shall give reflects an antitheatricality in the Shakespeare text. By calling that text "antitheatrical" I mean that it throws into question all the dramatic structures—narrative, episode, scene, character, and body—that theatrical performance privileges and the author of Shakespeare's plays clearly loves. I include among these structures the political and historical scenarios as embodiments of the patriarchal ideology with its two axes of hierarchy and orderly succession. I shall read the critique of drama and theater politically as a critique of that ideology, but what I am chiefly interested in is its relation not to the politics of the state but to that of father/son conflicts. I therefore view psychoanalytic, political, and dramatico-theatrical interpretation as closely intertwined strands of a single activity.

Mimesis is the common representational principle informing the organization of genealogical and hierarchic relationships, and of relationships among the text, the dramatic narrative, and theatrical performance. Thus I assume the text to be performing a critique of mimesis—and of its own mimetic status—in the very act of producing a mimesis. In exploring the critique I shall not bother with its possible relevance for allegories of the playwright's literary or psychological development. I prefer to seek within the dramatic community and its generational conflicts for the motives that lead to the production and critique of mimetic structures. What regulative and representational functions do these structures fulfill in relation to the father/son conflicts depicted in the *Henriad*? And since "in the *Henriad*" here means in the language of the play as it offers itself directly to readers rather than to actors, what functions do those structures fulfill in relation to the text?

I consider these two questions to be the same question, and I shall respond to it by exploring, in the interpretations that follow, a particular hypothesis: that Shakespeare's mimetic structures—theater, drama, and the narrative sequences they represent—are related to the text as manifest to latent contents; they are explicitly and conspicuously presented as displaced, condensed, and dramatized visualizations of latent textual meanings they thereby repress. This hypothesis will now be tested by excavating from the text of the first act of *Richard II* the shadowy evidence of the first major father/son conflict in the *Henriad.*

In the opening scenes of *Richard II,* the inflation of speech is no more conspicuous than the silences it constitutes as hidden behind it. Participants within the drama share with audiences and readerships an uneasy awareness that the ceremonially dramatic but otherwise non-committal language pushes much into the background, that ritual speech is being used to hide, mystify, or justify other motives than those expressed, and that no one knows exactly what those motives may be—least of all, perhaps, in some cases, those whose motives they are. Since the characters seem for the most part to be maneuvering in the dark, it may be risky to venture into one of the more charged and salient pockets of silence, the one that encloses what goes on between John of Gaunt and his son. That pocket is peripheral to the more central one enclosing what goes on between Richard and Bolingbroke; but since both pockets are mediated, or set off, or circumscribed, by the more accessible relationship between Richard and Gaunt, I shall observe due caution and begin there. The Gaunt/Bolingbroke relation remains a mystery throughout the *Henriad.* Bolingbroke's obsession with his relation to Richard crops up frequently in the *Henry IV* plays, and his revisionary retrospects afford at least limited access to what went on (or goes on) in *Richard II.* The relation between Gaunt and Richard is resolved with considerable stridency by the time act 2, scene 1 of the first play is over.

The general tenor of Richard's attitude toward Gaunt may be caught by trying to listen with Gaunt's ears to Richard's opening words:

> Old John of Gaunt, time-honoured Lancaster,
> Hast thou according to thy oath and band
> Brought hither Henry Herford thy bold son,
> Here to make good the boist'rous late appeal,
> Which then our leisure would not let us hear,
> Against the Duke of Norfolk, Thomas Mowbray?
>
> GAUNT: I have, my liege.
>
> (1.1.1–7)

The chiasmic patterning of name–title–title–name in the first and last lines works to Gaunt's detriment, since the last line lacks modifiers which Richard so pointedly uses in the first. The blunt and familiar opening, "Old John of Gaunt," edges the elegant variation that follows it with faint sarcasm. Richard pushes on the tonal difference between personal and ritual address, converts apposition into opposition, makes the second epithet sound like a euphemistic or mystified equivalent of the first. Then, turning from father to son, his alliterative coupling of "bold" with "boist'rous" reduces the ambivalent first term to its negative connotation: under the pressure of the meanings of "boisterous" (rough, coarse, clamorous, unskillful) "bold" shifts from "fearless" or "confident" to "presumptuous" or "forward." At the same time the combination of "son" and "boist'rous" tends to diminish Bolingbroke—to *boy* him—and to stress Gaunt's responsibility for his son's good behavior.

In the lines that follow the opening exchange, Richard continues to press on Gaunt's role as surety:

> RICHARD: Tell me, moreover, hast thou sounded him,
> If he appeal the Duke on ancient malice,
> Or worthily as a good subject should
> On some known ground of treachery in him?
> GAUNT: As near as I could sift him on that argument,
> On some apparent danger seen in him,
> Aim'd at your Highness, no inveterate malice.
> (1.1.8–14)

Although Richard's questions are clearly ceremonial, and therefore rhetorical, he puts them to aggressive use not merely in picking away at Gaunt's responsibility for the good faith of the appeal but also in trying to elicit a response that will reveal the extent of the knowledge, and perhaps complicity, Gaunt shares with his son. The response is evasive: not "*known* ground of treachery" but "*apparent* danger seen." The measured, heavily stopped blank verse of Gaunt's vague reply expresses the care he takes to dissociate himself from any appearance of complicity or knowledge. We hear much in later scenes about his view of Richard and England, but never a word about his relation to Bolingbroke's appeal—or, for that matter, about his relation to Bolingbroke. This is the subject which the following textual excavation aims to elucidate.

Bolingbroke prefaces his accusation of Mowbray with words in which, as the Arden editor observes, he "takes care to explain . . . the purity of his motives":

In the devotion of a subject's love,
Tend'ring the precious safety of my prince,
And free from other misbegotten hate,
Come I appellant to this princely presence.
(1.1.31–34)

While "other misbegotten hate" answers to Richard's "ancient malice" and thus apparently has Mowbray as its object, the vagueness of both phrases gives them a wider sweep, for in the background of the appeal lies the murder of Gloucester which is the climactic and most heavily stressed of the three articles in Bolingbroke's accusations: "misbegotten hate" may refer to the family feud and the motive for revenge.

In the rhetorical climax of his accusation, Bolingbroke asserts that Gloucester's blood,

like sacrificing Abel's, cries
Even from the tongueless caverns of the earth
To me for justice and rough chastisement;
And, by the glorious worth of my descent,
This arm shall do it, or this life be spent.
(1.1.104–8)

His generational logic is less shaky than it seems, for why should Gloucester's blood be like the archetypal murdered *brother's,* and why should it cry to *him* to be God's surrogate in this affair, unless he is replacing the father whose consenting silence amounts to symbolic fratricide, and whose "unwilling tongue" (1.3.245) diminishes "the glorious worth" of Bolingbroke's descent from Edward III? It is to these lines that Richard/Cain responds: "How high a pitch his resolution soars!" (l. 109). A few lines later, assuring Mowbray of his impartiality, he redefines the lineal scheme to his own advantage:

Were he my brother, nay, my kingdom's heir,
As he is but my father's brother's son,
Now by my sceptre's awe I make a vow,
Such neighbour nearness to our sacred blood
Should nothing privilege him
(1.1.116–20)

As Kittredge observes, the second line is a "slighting antithesis to 'my kingdom's heir.' " Though the derogation of Gaunt is here only a move in the game of lineal checkers, the opening words of the play had already begun to establish Richard's disdain for his uncle, and this impression is situationally reinforced shortly after when Gaunt participates in the tactic Richard employs to frustrate Bolingbroke's justice. In jingling rhymes whose flippancy sharpens the calculated tone of affront, Richard makes Gaunt share the onus of his arbitrary interruption of the ritual: "Good uncle, let this end where it begun; / We'll calm the Duke of Norfolk, you your son" (ll. 158–59). Gaunt complies with a disingenuous aphorism that avails itself of Richard's opening, "Old John of Gaunt," to activate the weakling's plea, senility: "To be a make-peace shall become my age. / Throw down, my son, the Duke of Norfolk's gage" (ll. 160–61).

Bolingbroke directs his bitter refusal to Richard, and continues insulting Mowbray, but if in reading his words we pretend once again to be listening with Gaunt's ears, we may feel that his son's sentiments towards those two targets are not entirely displaced:

> O God defend my soul from such deep sin!
> Shall I seem crest-fallen in my father's sight?
> Or with pale beggar-fear impeach my height
> Before this out-dar'd dastard? Ere my tongue
> Shall wound my honour with such feeble wrong,
> Or sound so base a parle, my teeth shall tear
> The slavish motive of recanting fear,
> And spit it bleeding in his high disgrace,
> Where shame doth harbour, even in Mowbray's face.
> (1.1.187–95)

The second line contains the only verbal acknowledgment of his father's presence made by Bolingbroke in this scene. It is ceremonially correct: he salutes the immediate source of "the glorious worth of my descent" and states his unwillingness to dishonor the source by displaying cowardice before his father's eyes. Nevertheless, this line gives the whole speech the capacity to strike daggers into any ears pretending to be Gaunt's.

Since Gaunt commanded the display, the ritual force of the rhetorical question changes to "shall I let my father have the satisfaction of watching me perform the base act he and Richard urged on me?" The question that follows may then be heard as intensifying the speaker's sense of outrage: "Is this what you ask me to do, lower my crest by impeaching my height with a display of fear?" The parallelism of the prepositional clauses that end each question places Gaunt and Mowbray in the same position. This adds interest to "out-dar'd": it does not characterize Mowbray's behavior, and as a ritual insult it does not have to, but it can be applied with some justice to Gaunt who, unwilling to avenge or speak up for his brother himself, seconded the king's attempt to frustrate Bolingbroke's appeal "for justice and rough chastisement." His son's refusal to be infected with this shameful fear-bred silence challenges Gaunt's self-imposed tonguelessness: the amputated tongue symbolizes the father's "feeble wrong" ("Ere my [father] / Shall wound my honour"), and the hyperbolic violence directed at this ritual surrogate is at once masked and enabled by the careful emphasis of the final clause, "even in Mowbray's face." This displacement effectively makes the speech self-referential, for Bolingbroke is spitting his challenge to Gaunt in Mowbray's face.

Our evidence for decoding the meant or unmeant messages one character receives from another's words comes from the meant or unmeant meaning transmitted through his own words. Gaunt's words to the Duchess, which follow almost immediately after Bolingbroke's speech, register an uneasiness that suggests he is belatedly directing toward her the kind of lame excuse he might wish to make toward his son; yet at the same time they register more aggressive feelings:

> Alas, the part I had in Woodstock's blood
> Doth more solicit me than your exclaims
> To stir against the butchers of his life;
> But since correction lieth in those hands
> Which made the fault that we cannot correct,
> Put we our quarrel to the will of heaven,
> Who, when they see the hours ripe on earth,
> Will rain hot vengeance on offenders' heads.
>
> (1.2.1–8)

Gaunt is very careful here with his plural forms and shifters, and though we immediately identify "the butchers," "those hands," and "offenders," "they" in line 7 is less obvious—what divine, angelic, or human avengers pluralize "the will of heaven"? When will they judge the time to be ripe? And into what saving community of "we" does the first person of lines 1–2 vanish? If the apocalyptic excuse is meant to suggest a more legitimately sanctioned revenge than his son's effort, and one from which Gaunt will be spared, what could that possibly be? The vagueness of "offenders," lacking the article that would link it more closely to particular "butchers" and "hands," implies something not less encompassing and remote than the psalmist's wish for fire and brimstone, or the Last Judgment; it measures the sense of justified helplessness Gaunt encodes in the "we" of line 5; hence according to the logic of his argument those who wrongly attempt correction will join the offenders at the general doom. In act 1, scene 1, he had heard his son say that he would make his challenge to Mowbray "good upon this earth, / O my divine soul answer it in heaven" (ll. 37–38), and buried in Gaunt's words to the Duchess is a protest against that arrogance.

The Duchess, however, does not let Gaunt slip off into the Elizabethan world picture, nor even into the sunset of his declining years: "Finds brotherhood in thee no sharper spur? / Hath love in thy old blood no living fire?" (ll. 9–10). She accuses him of something very like the "pale beggar-fear" and "feeble wrong" spat out by Bolingbroke:

> thou dost consent
> In some large measure to thy father's death
> In that thou seest thy wretched brother die,
> Who was the model of thy father's life.
> Call it not patience, Gaunt, it is despair;
> In suff'ring thus thy brother to be slaught'red,
> Thou showest the naked pathway to thy life,
> Teaching stern murder how to butcher thee.
> That which in mean men we intitle patience
> Is pale cold cowardice in noble breasts.
> What shall I say? to safeguard thine own life,
> The best way is to venge my Gloucester's death.
> (1.2.25–36)

In these words Gaunt could well hear Bolingbroke's allusion to symbolic fratricide repeated as a direct accusation, intensified by conversion to symbolic parricide.

He defends himself with an aggressive restatement of the Tudor ideology:

> God's is the quarrel—for God's substitute,
> His deputy anointed in His sight,
> Hath caus'd his death; the which if wrongfully,
> Let heaven revenge, for I may never lift
> An angry arm against His minister.
> (1.2.37–41)

These words both acknowledge his feeble wrong and register the need to justify it more fully by rejecting the Duchess's appeal to the vendetta ethic. The concluding lines use the Tudor theory to rationalize his own "patience," but they also imply a criticism of Bolingbroke's impatient arm. To Dover Wilson they seemed to "condemn in advance the usurpation of his son . . . after his death," but I think the observed connection to Bolingbroke is strengthened by being shifted from the prospective mode of dramatic irony to the retrospective mode of structural irony.

When Gaunt suggests that the Duchess should direct her complaint to "God, the widow's champion and defence," her reply is definitive, and Gaunt makes no answer to it:

> Why then, I will. Farewell, old Gaunt.
> Thou goest to Coventry, there to behold
> Our cousin Herford and fell Mowbray fight.
> O, sit my husband's wrongs on Herford's spear,
> That it may enter butcher Mowbray's breast!
> Or if misfortune miss the first career,
> Be Mowbray's sins so heavy in his bosom
> That they may break his foaming courser's back
> And throw the rider headlong in the lists,
> A caitive recreant to my cousin Herford!
> Farewell, old Gaunt; thy sometimes brother's wife
> With her companion, grief, must end her life.
> GAUNT: Sister, farewell; I must to Coventry,
> As much good stay with thee as go with me!
>
> (1.2.44–57)

The Duchess refuses to call Bolingbroke Gaunt's son. In the first of her three references to him he is "*Our* cousin"—she shares him equally with Gaunt in a general classificatory relation—and by the third, at line 53, her possession has become singular. This shift destabilizes the modifier in the next line: we may read it either as "thy brother's sometimes wife" or as "the wife of thy sometimes brother," cut off from Gaunt not only by his death but also by the recreancy that would leave "sacrificing Abel" unavenged, i.e., "you are no longer of 'our faith,' and our extended kin group is now represented by our cousin, not by you; he has assumed your lapsed responsibility." But since the Duchess has already described that lapse as a wrong done to her husband, the implication is even stronger. "O, sit my husband's wrongs on Herford's spear": to replace Gaunt and to redress his wrong is to challenge him to combat. Once again, the "recreant" Mowbray is a ritual scapegoat, and the violent imagery of trial by combat provides a hyperbolic image, a melodramatic outlet, for the displaced expression of sentiments that might be less easy to entertain toward Gaunt.

The argument I have excavated from the tongueless caverns of the Duchess's language is that Bolingbroke has replaced—indeed, displaced—his father as the true son of Edward III and brother of Gloucester, and that some defensive and even resentful recognition of the argument is embedded in Gaunt's language. When I read "Hath love in thy old blood no living fire?" I recall and refocus Gaunt's "To be a make-peace shall become my age," seeing it now tinged by rueful and bitter, if resigned, acknowledgment of the trimmer's role he has assumed in others' eyes—tinged also by a more aggressive complement: "To be a troublemaker becomes his youth."

The Duchess names Gaunt four times in this scene: she calls him "Gaunt" twice in her opening speech when she still hopes to persuade him to action, but switches to "old Gaunt" after he has referred her to God, the widow's champion, and she turns instead to Herford for succor. I think the contexts in which the Duchess, Richard, and Gaunt himself refer to his age—whether in epithets, descriptions, or puns—almost always skewer the reference on the sharp sword of the father/son interaction: when his authority over Bolingbroke is invoked or being called into question (1.1.1, 160, 162–63); when—as here—Bolingbroke's challenge is contrastively related to his own ideologically toned evasions; and when, after being party to his son's banishment, he complains to Richard that it will hasten his death (1.3.216–32).

Under the pressure of these contexts and their language, "old" and "gaunt" become Gaunt's defensive weapons in the struggle between father and son that marks the passage of patriarchal authority from predecessor to successor, aged to young, old to new—it would be better to say the passage of phallic power, since my excavation leads me to conclude that the play's language characterizes Gaunt not only as pleading impotence, and not only as accused of it, but also as symbolically "castrated" by Bolingbroke's challenge. And this is the conclusion I want to carry as a hypothesis into the third scene of act 1: Bolingbroke's presence and behavior are a standing rebuke to Gaunt; he feels accused and challenged, replaced and excelled, by his son; Bolingbroke's innuendoes in 1.1, reinforced by the Duchess's charges in 1.2, point toward a father who has been "deposed," or self-deposed, having allowed his son to "usurp" his place and function in the generational order; thus to see and be seen by his son ("in my father's sight") may not cause him unmitigated joy, and this occasions another speculation: will it cause him unmitigated grief to be relieved of that presence?

"As much good stay with thee as go with me": the limp sentiment with which Gaunt takes his leave hardly suggests that he is any more eager to rush off to Coventry than he is to linger on and hear the Duchess talk about it. The contrast to Bolingbroke is driven home in the opening lines of 1.3:

> MARSHALL: My Lord Aumerle, is Harry Herford arm'd?
> AUMERLE: Yea, at all points, and longs to enter in.

Bolingbroke does not immediately appear, however; Mowbray enters and speaks first. Ritual purists complain that the appellant should have preceded the defendant into the lists. But the reversed order makes possible an interesting variation in Richard's two requests to the Marshall to administer the oath of justice. For Mowbray, he uses these words: "swear him in the justice of his cause." But for Bolingbroke the formula is significantly altered, and I think the significance is underlined by its contrast to the earlier request: "Depose him in the justice of his cause." Reading the word that names the central action of the play, I succumb to the charm of several temptations. First, of course, the pun invites a proleptic interpretation—as if Richard already sees Bolingbroke crowned and pronounces a curse ("Let him be deposed") that nevertheless reflects awareness of his own unjust regime. This implies a second alternative, "Depose *me* in the justice of his cause," from which I slide helplessly into the pleasure of imagining either or both statements as expressions of Gaunt's dilemma: "if my son is 'deposed' by Mowbray, his cause will be proved unjust, *ergo,* I shall be justified, but if his cause is just, I am 'deposed.' "

A similar temptation is dropped in my path by Richard's leavetaking of Bolingbroke:

> We will descend and fold him in our arms.
> Cousin of Herford, as thy cause is right,
> So be thy fortune in this royal fight!
> Farewell, my blood; which if to-day thou shed,
> Lament we may, but not revenge thee dead.
> (1.3.54–58)

In the first line I see not only a foreshadowing of the deposition scene but a condensed visualization of Richard's latent project as it unfolds through the play, here displaced to the physical circumstance of a ceremonial gesture. The rhythm accentuates the *will* to descend; the second phrase is a kinesic hyperbole that mimes the desire coupling Richard to Bolingbroke in their dance toward deposition and regicide, and toward the subsequent regime, when the embrace gradually becomes a stranglehold. This line chimes with "Depose" and with the odd reference to "royal fight" as an element of the proleptic rhetoric threading glints of the latent project through the first and third scenes of the play.

The second couplet adds another element: Richard's message is that if Bolingbroke loses he will unjustly have shed the "high blood" his royal kinsman shares, but his language also lets the alternate message, "if you kill me," flicker briefly before us. In the final line, the alert excavator might discern another displacement. While the statement is sardonic in Richard's mouth—as if he might be expected to avenge his kinsman and has to explain that he won't—it crisply epitomizes the attitude Gaunt expressed in 1.2: "Lament" = "Alas, the part I had in Woodstock's blood"; "but not revenge" = "I may never lift / An angry arm," since Mowbray will have proved to be heaven's minister.

In the balanced duplicity of these lines Richard flaunts his mastery of the rhetorical tease. He (con)descends to favor Bolingbroke with a hug and a word of tepid encouragement (by the judicial logic of trial by combat, "as" in line 55 must mean "if," not "since"), then devotes the last line and a half to harping on his possible defeat. Rhymes, end-stopping, and echoing caesuras add bite to his wicked tongue—the finality, certainty, and witty detachment of aphoristic or recited speech. This is political, not merely poetic, mastery. Even as he folds the successor-to-be in his arms, he sends the usurper-to-be off with a dry-eyed mock. Bolingbroke parries the mock in answering couplets that are more forceful but less balanced and assured:

> O, let no noble eye profane a tear
> For me, if I be gor'd with Mowbray's spear!
> As confident as is the falcon's flight
> Against a bird, do I with Mowbray fight.
> (1.3.59–62)

This begins well with "profane a tear"; the lament would be profaned not only by his unworthiness but also because it would indubitably be feigned. Yet the expansive energy of his heroic clichés flags suddenly at the end of each enjambment. The falcon comes down on its prey more confidently than the figure does on "a bird." The trajectory of Bolingbroke's career, its brief upward surge and long anticlimax, is epitomized in this rhythm. His real contest is not the physical encounter with Mowbray but the verbal encounter with Richard, and, behind that, the silent encounter with Gaunt. The putative referent of the words—the anticipated fight with Mowbray—is actually the signifier of the present power struggle that goes on, and will continue to go on, within the "fair designs" of the rhetorical lists.

After two unrhymed lines of farewell to Richard and Aumerle, and a summary couplet broadcasting his self-assurance, Bolingbroke winds up for the climax of his speech—his farewell to Gaunt—with an odd simile: "Lo, as at English feasts, so I regreet / The daintiest last, to make the end most sweet" (1.3.67–68). The figure implies that these "ceremonious" farewells and salutes are things to be savored, things to be consumed. The farewell salute to Gaunt will be the tastiest morsel. Bolingbroke's emphasis is on rhetorical pleasure and performance rather than on the illocutionary force of the sentiment; he will confect a filial dessert of sweetly end-stopped pieties. Yet, once again, the language writhes out of his control and serves up a more disconcerting message:

> O thou, the earthly author of my blood,
> Whose youthful spirit in me regenerate
> Doth with a twofold vigour lift me up
> To reach at victory above my head,
> Add proof unto mine armour with thy prayers,
> And with thy blessings steel my lance's point,
> That it may enter Mowbray's waxen coat,
> And furbish new the name of John a Gaunt,
> Even in the lusty haviour of his son.
>
> (1.3.69–77)

The frame or crust of this trifle is a request for blessing; the filler is a respectful *æmulatio*. But from under the mock modesty of the fourth line something interesting begins to bubble forth. "To reach . . . above my head" can hardly refer to victory over Mowbray; whatever the speaker intends, the words are steeled (or stolen) by another sky-aspiring proleptic allusion: they point toward Richard. Then, with "furbish," they become more abrasive as their lance passes almost too easily from Mowbray's waxen coat to Gaunt's rusty name. [Peter] Ure makes a good case for preferring the Quarto's "furbish" to the Folio's "furnish"; "Besides its more general meaning of 'clean up,' *furbish* means 'scour the rust from armour' . . . so Gaunt's 'name' (honour, repute) is also his armour, and the metaphor continues the references to arms and armour in the preceding lines." But it also joins with "new" to scratch away at the film of self-apology Gaunt has coated his name with—"*Old* John of *Gaunt*." It is the *former* spirit of Gaunt's youth that Bolingbroke invokes to help the falcon soar to the height of his heavenly author's quarrel; a spirit that died and now revives only in the "lusty haviour" of the son whose angry arm will "scour the rust" from his earthly author's (and his family's) once untarnished honor.

Bolingbroke's English confection thus concludes as a challenge to Gaunt to support his cause: the son's victory will clear his father's name. The name-clearing problem places Gaunt in a classic double bind, since he also seems to want a clear name in the court's eyes and those of God's anointed deputy. This problem comes into focus after the interruption when Richard reminds him that his "tongue a party-verdict gave" to his son's banishment (1.3.234). Gaunt's rueful reaction to the verdict and to his share in it is troubled by his strident protest of nonresponsibility. But I think it is also troubled by the deceptively truistic distinction with which he justifies himself:

> You urg'd me as a judge, but I had rather
> You would have bid me argue like a father.
> O, had it been a stranger, not my child,
> To smooth his fault I should have been more mild.
> A partial slander sought I to avoid,
> And in the sentence my own life destroy'd.
> Alas, I look'd when some of you should say
> I was too strict to make mine own away;
> But you gave leave to my unwilling tongue
> Against my will to do myself this wrong.
> (1.3.237–46)

The first couplet says that if he had been arguing as a father he would have been more mild. The second couplet says that if he had been arguing as a nonfather he would have been more mild. The first couplet implies that he argued as a nonfather in order to avoid the charge of prejudice. The second couplet implies that being less mild in order to avoid the charge of prejudice is acting like a father. But consider also the following variation: "Because it was no stranger but my child, / I could not smooth his fault or be more mild." This more directly conveys the message that the partiality of the loving father is not toward any child but toward a guilty child. Gaunt acknowledges his son's fault, confesses to a father's impulse to overlook it (only a "child," after all), and goes on to lament the strictness of the loyal and obedient subject forced to suppress the impulse in the interest of justice. In this parable, the primary focus of self-presentation is on the trials of the good father. Gaunt is smoothing faults all around—Richard's, his own—and the smoothness penetrates the syrupy rhymes and rhythms of his speech.

What the speech actually suppresses is the fear and guilt of the bad father, who pleads the avoidance of partiality to cover other motives for being less mild to a son than to a stranger. He blames others for letting himself destroy his life and for not telling him "I was too strict to make mine own away." The elliptical strain of this phrase betrays the pressure of his not mentioning what he is doing to his "child": insofar as "make . . . away" is apposite to "my own life destroy'd," it means "do away with"; but insofar as it refers to Bolingbroke's exile it means "send away." In the blurring together of these senses, "mine own" opens up to include not only his upright self-sacrifice but also the sacrifice of his son that enables him to avoid a partial slander. "Mine own" justifies both sacrifices, because it suggests that his son, like his life, is his possession, to dispose with as he judges right. This judgment, he explains, is the source of his grief. Yet further reflection will show that it is also the effect of his guilt, which it reinforces.

Since Gaunt's conversation with the Duchess established his interest in making himself and others believe that it is wrong to oppose the king, we can imagine him seeing Bolingbroke's de facto challenge to Richard through the medium of Mowbray as a fault in which he could easily be implicated as an accomplice to a plot fomented by the Gloucester faction. This changes the import of "partial slander" from "accusation of leniency" to "accusation of complicity": it would have been easier for him to smooth the fault of a stranger whose questionable motives did not glance at him. What could make his party-verdict doubly painful is his sense that he has sacrificed his son to clear himself. His behavior constitutes a betrayal of Bolingbroke and his cause; worse than that, it expresses a desire to betray his son. He looked in vain for others to temper this ignoble impulse. The unstable syntax of the final couplet betrays the effect of their failure. Construed as a redundant negative construction, it says that both he and his tongue were unwilling to do himself the injury of voting for his son's exile, or to inflict on his son the injury he ignobly desired to inflict. But construed as an antithetical construction—"[my unwilling tongue] / Against [my will to do myself this wrong]"—it says that he had a will, a desire, to do this wrong, that he was unwilling to actualize the desire in speech, but that Richard's urging prevailed upon him.

The conclusion of this strenuous excavation of Gaunt's lines is that they betray his fear of being contaminated by Bolingbroke's action; his reluctant agreement to the sentence of exile in response to that fear; the desire to defeat the son who challenges him; the guilt occasioned in him by that desire and by an agreement that sacrifices his son's interest to his own; and the attempt to assuage that guilt by blaming his party-verdict on others, an attempt that could only increase the corrosive power of self-despite. What destroys his life, then, what makes him gaunt for the grave, is not merely grief at being separated from his son, perhaps forever, but guilt at having willed to do his son that wrong. On Bolingbroke's side, the father/son conflict is concealed, enabled, exacerbated by a double displacement: from Gaunt to Richard to Mowbray; from father to king to peer. Mowbray serves as the medium in which are condensed Bolingbroke's darker purpose, to accuse the king, and his darkest purpose, to rebuke his father.

The centrality of this conflict in the *Henriad* is obvious and has often been noted, but never with reference to Gaunt and Bolingbroke. As I stated at the beginning of the essay, my purpose in excavating their relationship has been to situate an interpretation in the most antitheatrical reaches of the text in order to position myself "outside" the politico-historical and dramatico-theatrical narrative privileged by stage-centered criticism. This positioning (or positing) allows me to interpret the emergence of that narrative in functional terms as a defensive transformation of latencies in the text, and to explore the dialectic by which Shakespeare represents the meaning of theatrical drama in those terms. I conclude with a brief reading of a passage that will open up onto a summary overview of the process I have been discussing.

Early in the play Richard commands the appearance of Bolingbroke and Mowbray in characteristically tortured syntax:

> Then call them to our presence; face to face,
> And frowning brow to brow, ourselves will hear
> The accuser and the accused freely speak.
>
> (1.1.15–17)

"Face to face, / And frowning brow to brow": leading off thus with a pair of unbound modifier phrases frees them up for serial redefinition. In a first fleeting mirage they seem to describe Richard confronting the other two as *his* antagonists and/or appellants. This gives way to a second when the strangely pluralized royal plural suggests that he confronts and/or accuses himself. Finally, the opposed selves are bound to their proper ritual representatives in line 17, and their proper ritualized representation in lines 18–19, an event celebrated with the play's first rhymed couplet: "High-stomach'd are they both and full of ire, / In rage, deaf as the sea, hasty as fire."

The shift in these six lines from enjambed, internally stopped blank verse to end-stressed rhymed verse reinforces the shift from uncertain syntax and rapidly changing impressions to the too predictable formulas of chivalric rhetoric, which in this case produces an oxymoronic relation between what is said and how it is said: the analogies of nature are clichés of art; the reported unruliness of the combatants is overruled by the measured rhythm of the report, by its discountable literary hyperboles. And there is a sense in which their rage will be as artificial and literary as the language, a sense in which the "report" is actually a self-fulfilling stage direction that prescribes the emotions and behavior appropriate to culturally prefabricated roles embedded in a certain institutional narrative. The rage will also be artificial because it will be ritually displaced and misdirected.

The shifts described above combine to mark the most fundamental process that structures this drama: the passage and transformation of conflict from the tongueless caverns of some "hidden imposthume" to the safety of the sanctioned artifice and "fair designs" of ritualized combat and behavior. In the *Henriad* the equivalents of Hamlet's phrase are, like his, carefully vague, as if keeping their distance from the miasma they fear to touch: "buried fear," "some other grief," "inward wars." The passage from this latent content to the manifest fictions of ritual embodiment is perfectly described by Lafew in *All's Well That Ends Well*: "we make trifles of terrors, ensconcing ourselves into seeming knowledge when we should submit ourselves to an unknown fear" (2.3.3ff.). A sconce is a fortress, and in *Richard II* the conspicuous trifles, the stiff and stilted formulas, of ritual are the palisades that impose quarantine against the miasma:

> I'll answer thee in any fair degree
> Or chivalrous design of knightly trial
> (1.1.80–81)

On pain of death, no person be so bold
Or daring-hardy as to touch the lists,
Except the marshall and such officers
Appointed to direct these fair designs.
(1.3.42–45)

The textual confusions buried in Richard's call to the combatants resonate with obscure, labile, and dangerous power struggles—rooted in fear, guilt, aggressivity, self-contempt, and Janus-faced desire—that defy closure and shun exposure; his final couplet visualizes the dramatic form in which they can find legitimate heroic expression and narrative resolution.

Trial by combat displaces, condenses, dramatizes, and thereby at once represses and represents such "inward wars" as those that divide a father from his son and from himself. Shakespeare's achievement lies in making the "fair designs" represent and be touched by the miasma they eschew. The prescribed rhetoric of ritual speech and action is shown to be inadequate to deal with or represent whatever "other grief" is buried in the language of the dramatic community. It is precisely its inadequacy, its parodic and artificial character, that lets the ritual function as a mode of concealment enabling the hidden struggles to continue. To borrow René Girard's terms, if trial by combat is a caricature of *differentiation,* Shakespeare presents it as such by encouraging us to search his text for the undifferentiating forces that produce the caricature as its instrument. Cutting across the differentiating boundaries of the nominal combatants and subjects of dispute, the text throws anamorphic shadows that bathe the empty glitter of ceremonial speech in a rich chiaroscuro.

Girard's distinction was formulated not for the analysis of a particular ritual but for all ritual, including what he refers to as the "surface play," and I have argued elsewhere that the surface play is the one privileged by theatrical performance. My concluding incautious generalizations are that the preceding comments on trial by combat apply to Shakespeare's representation of the "fair designs" of theatrical performance on its audience; apply to dramatic fiction, whether staged or not; apply to any transformational interaction between the excavated meanings of the text and the speech assigned to names we conventionally reify and imagine as persons. They apply wherever language is distributed among the embodied subjects who speak it. The *meta*morphosis of text into bodies produces conspicuous *ana*morphosis that has the same function and effects as those of the "fair designs" of trial by combat. Socially or culturally produced structures of embodiment—of presences, subjects, characters, roles, individuals—are quarantines against the "discourse of the Other" (Lacan) that smokes the edges of clear visualization and ambiguates simple location. The plastic design behind that mode of production is to *pre-vent* "bad humors" by providing identities and stories the actors can live with, narratives that enable them to discharge those humors while preserving unawareness and self-esteem. The embodiment of presence is thus the building of Lafew's sconce.

Shakespeare's text, then, is not the representation of drama per se but rather the representation of its construction *out of* the text's discourse of the Other and *against* that discourse—the representation and, in the positive sense, the critique of the self-concealing motivational conditions of embodiment. Insofar as theatrical performance is the ritual reinforcement of the drive to embodiment, its actualization in living bodies, it intensifies the defensive flight of drama from text, imposing itself on the contours of drama like a template that masks its underlying textuality. Shakespeare's metatheatrical critique of theater is, as we know, contained within his metadramatic critique of drama. These are enabling, not inhibiting, critiques: they support his production of dramatic fictions and theatrical performances in a transgressive manner, that is, by clearly signaling their limits, laying bare the motives behind their production, adumbrating a textual dimension at once implicit in them and beyond them. To represent performed drama *as* a flight from text is to enrich it with the transcendent fringe of meanings, the signifying nothing conspicuously concealed by the sound and fury of the words, conspicuously frustrated by the splendors of embodiment. The fury, splendor, and frustration can be experienced together only in performance; we have to feel the presence and pressure of the theatrical template, submit to its fair designs, in order to measure both *its* power and the shadowy counterforce of the power it represses. The politics of that repression cannot be borne home to us in any other way. But the fury, splendor, frustration, and politics can only be understood and evaluated by the excavation that psychoanalyzes the text.

The Typical Register in Shakespeare's *Richard II*

Susan Wells

Let us begin by situating the text historically, orienting ourselves to the terrain of the play's typical relations. We can safely assert, relying on modern historians, that Shakespeare's period saw the development of something like a modern state in England. The English state changed from the household establishment of the king to an autonomous structure, capable in theory of fully governing the realm and organized according to relatively bureaucratic and rational, rather than personal and customary, norms. For Shakespeare, writing in such a period, the dynastic wars were a politically charged subject, recalling the crucible in which this state had been formed. And for us, a modern audience, the construction of the state form that even now governs us is of more than antiquarian interest. Let us take, then, that state as a common location, a piece of shared ground from which we can begin to survey the horizon of the play, onto which we can summon the images it invokes. Such a procedure allows us to integrate our understanding of the ideological apparatus available to Shakespeare with our immediate experience of the play. In the forty years of historical commentary on Shakespeare's history cycle, quite a few features of this apparatus have been identified, from the orthodox chain of being posited by Tillyard through the investigations of Machiavellian statecraft or the redaction of the Elizabethan political consensus proposed by various revisionist theorists. If this information aids us in recreating the world of the play,

---

From *The Dialectics of Representation*. © 1985 by the Johns Hopkins University Press, Baltimore/London.

it does not also make the play's world our own. As Robert Weimann puts it, the task of interpretation must take into account the contexts of both writer and reader: "For the literary historian and critic the question, then, is not whether to accept both worlds as points of reference, but rather *how* to relate them so as to obtain their maximum dimension . . . to have as much of the historical significance and as much of the contemporary meaning merged into a new unity."

How then does the state shape the relations of representation in *Richard II*? The state, first, is a "new thing" within the universe of the play. Instead of being assimilated and naturalized by political ideology, the state is a scandal, a stumbling block in the way of routine observation, a thing to be explained. Consider, by way of contrast, Steinbeck's *Grapes of Wrath,* where the activity of the state is transparent and unproblematic. The Elizabethan writer faced the problem of reshaping the conventions of chronicle history, heroic drama, and moral interlude to the new form of the state. Shakespeare's solution to this problem provokes us, as readers, to rethink the state, since the normal tropes in which realist literature recuperates the state as a natural structure are absent from *Richard II.* In its representation of the state, then, *Richard II* can challenge us, say something new to us.

The state is also a virtually unique place in modern discourse for examining questions about community, about the nature of public life and its relation to private life. It is thus a vehicle for discussing the proper relations of individuals and groups. Marx pointed out long ago that a certain alienation and distortion are implicit in this process, whereby "every common interest" is "straightway severed from society, counterposed to it as a higher, general interest snatched from the activity of society's members themselves." But this very alienation establishes a certain congruence between the state and the typical register of representation: the state is a concrete structure representing a range of individual experiences. Our horizon, then, conjoins with that of the play's original audience, who saw the sovereign-subject relation as both pattern and source of every relation between a superior and an inferior—and thus, for all important social relations. For the Elizabethan, the sovereign-subject relation mobilized all the terms in the lexicon of power, from the totalized language of awe in prescribed homilies: "so doth God himself in the same Scriptures sometime vouchsafe to communicate his name with earthly princes, terming them Gods," to the more intimate terms of Stafford's speech to the Council of the North: "Princes are to be the indulgent nursing fathers to their people. . . . Verily these are those mutual intelligences of love and protection descending and loyalty ascending which should pass . . . between the king and his people."

If the Elizabethans saw social institutions in terms of personal relationships, we see communal relationships among persons in terms of social institutions. Thus, by a strange spiraling of ideology, the relations between Renaissance sovereign and subject provide us with ideological forms complementary to our own: the gaps and vacancies in our ideology are indicated by what has been made explicit in theirs. The state, which is both an institution and the personal tool of the sovereign, thus provides, in Henry James's famous phrase, a circle within which social relations appear to end, a circle we share with the play's original audiences, and that circumscribes the play's typical register.

The relations between subject and sovereign, or more specifically, among Richard II, Bolingbroke, and other characters in the play, thus becomes representations, both of the shifting relations of public and private life and of the scope, power, and impersonality of the new monarchy. Shakespeare organizes this representation in a number of formal patterns, from the archaic allegory of the garden scene to the Senecan deposition scene. The traditional forms of chronicle play, moral interlude, and royal tragedy describe a monarchy that could no longer be traditional.

However, *Richard II* is not a simple conflict between archaic and modern state structures, with Richard personifying an attractive but doomed traditional monarchy and Bolingbroke the rising but humanly inhospitable modern state. Such a representational structure would be simply allegorical, and *Richard II*—unlike, say, *Richard III*—has a typical register demanding enough to subordinate the allegorical strains of the play. Rather, both characters display complex relations to the problems posed by the modern state, so that those problems are mediated by intersubjectivity. Richard tries to solve the problems of a modern state with the tools of traditional rule; he ends by retreating to the private, to a sphere of significance "outside" the state, a location for intimacy and interiority. Bolingbroke, on the other hand, challenges the state on the basis of his private "right"; his subjectivity becomes an instrument of rule.

This representation is not a mirror for princes, or for magistrates; it is rather a translation of political problems into terms accessible to the intersubjective imagination. The varying accommodations of Richard and Bolingbroke demonstrate different possibilities of the situation. Richard is unable to master the forms of the new state: he continues to rely on familial and customary forms of rule, forms that always fail him as he undertakes modern projects. The institutions of customary society, arrayed before us in the first scene—the ducal council, ceremonial trial by combat, the oath—rest on relations of consent and of mutual obligation. They do not cohere with the impersonal, almost bureaucratic, relations of authority that characterize an omnicompetent state on its way to becoming an absolute monarchy—in Elizabethan terms, an imperium. Such dissonance would be only a stylistic problem were not Richard also engaged in acts that required all the powers of the developed state. His farming of the realm for taxes would have reminded the Elizabethan audience of Henry VIII's misnamed "Amicable Grant," another blank-charter tax that had excited so much resistance it had to be repealed. He is engaged in the perennial task of subduing the stateless Irish to the nascent empire, and he keeps the style of an absolute monarch; he is blamed for "too great a court and liberal largess." He attempts to impose upon his most powerful vassals the forms of equality before law observed in a modern state: "He [Bolingbroke] is our subject, Mowbray, so art thou" (1.1.32), thus endangering the familial forms that shore up his slender support. Richard, then, is trying to be two different kinds of king, a customary feudal king and the ruler of an imperium. The contradictions of this enterprise force him doubly into the sphere of the private—he treats the realm as his private property ("landlord of England art thou, not king," 2.1.113), and in his monologues, Richard expresses the only private subjectivity available in the play. We will return to this theme.

In the character of Richard, four heterogeneous elements are conjoined: the modern state, customary society, private property, and private subjectivity. Richard, of course, cannot reconcile the contradictions among these elements. But in his passage from public life to private life, Richard presents the contradictions to us as a series of subjective experiences. By mediating these problems through the character of Richard, the play simultaneously invites us to investigate these themes and assures us that they will bear investigation. If Richard can live out the troubled relation between the state and customary society, then surely we can think out that relation. Rather than being subordinated to a series of allegorical categories, the characters of *Richard II* mediate the contradictory categories in which the play organizes lived experience, so that political and cultural processes are presented in their intersubjective forms.

Bolingbroke also mediates these contradictory elements, but in quite a different way. He is a magnate; his private grievance—Gloucester's death—thereby derives public force. But in the context of the omnicompetent state, Bolingbroke is only another subject. He appears initially as an embodiment of archaic forms, a champion going into combat "lusty, young, and cheerly drawing breath" (1.3.66). Later, as bare abstract subject, he will defend primogeniture as a universal law. Paradoxically, it is this double quality of Bolingbroke—carrier of customary privilege and isolated individual struggling for his due—that allows him to justify himself in respect both to the rights of customary society and to the duties of a modern subject. His struggle for his own becomes a common cause. Thus, when Bolingbroke asserts, "I am a subject, / and I challenge law" (2.3.134–35), his location within two systems of subordination gives his modest claim sovereign force. Bolingbroke's skillful exploitation of his dangerous position contrasts with Richard's bumbling, since Richard cannot manage even so public an obligation as the Irish wars without seeming greedy for private profit. And, while Richard's personal subjectivity threatens to absorb his ceremonial decorum, Bolingbroke invests himself with that glamour of power that was to the Elizabethans an attribute of royalty. Richard, at a crucial moment, is reduced to a body:

> throw away respect,
> Tradition, form, and ceremonious duty;
> For you have but mistook me all this while.
> I live with bread like you, feel want, taste grief,
> Need friends. Subjected thus,
> How can you say to me I am a king?
>
> (3.2.172–77)

But Bolingbroke is able to use his body as weapon and advertisement; Richard observes his "courtship to the common people," as he goes "wooing poor craftsmen with the craft of smiles" (1.4.28).

In the final act of the play, both kings are isolated: Richard at Promfret Castle and Bolingbroke at court. These twin images of isolated individuality invite us to reflect on the relations of royal dominance and subordination that constitute the play's public and private worlds. And since we, who do not live in a world ruled by kings, do live in a world where even the most intimate relations are determined by public norms of power, these reflections open the play to us, open our lives for us, allow us to interpret the play as a typical representation of the relations that shape our own world.

It is not surprising, then, that critical responses to this play, and to the history plays in general, have reflected quite faithfully twentieth-century understandings about the state. Traditional critics like Tillyard, writing at mid-century, preoccupied with notions of order, saw insurgent readings of the history plays as anachronistic and unhistorical. In Tillyard's memorable formula, the "delusion" that Hal was wrong to cast off Falstaff "will probably be accounted for, in later years, through the facts of history. The sense of security created in nineteenth century England by the predominance of the British navy induced men to rate that very security too cheaply and to exalt the instinct of rebellion above its legitimate station." Like Tillyard, New Critics were preoccupied with the question of how individual integrity could be protected from the distortions of politics. Both of these concerns respond to the problems raised by fascism and world war: anxiety for the future of parliamentary democracies and a profound distrust of mass movements and mass enthusiasms. Critics of the sixties, on the other hand, turned from the celebration of authority to a critique of artifice and an investigation of personal politics, echoing the central topics of contemporaneous political discourse. And a critic writing in the eighties, Gordon Ross Smith, reads the history plays as a complaint against violence, corruption, and waste—a post-Watergate Henriad, by way of *Sixty Minutes*. There is nothing magical in this play that makes it relevant to so many historical situations. Rather, it is because *Richard II* phrases its investigation of the basic relations of political domination as a conflict between two discrete individuals that these relations are mobilized, unfolded, mediated in different ways. And since such mediating devices are presented intersubjectively, responses to the characters in this play can simultaneously reflect deeply subjective concerns and lend themselves to "objective" formulation. The most common way to take up a new hermeneutic stance toward *Richard II*, then, has been to call for a reexamination of the historical record, to announce a new, more faithful, recreation of the "background" of the play.

Let us consider again how the play itself treats the theme of subjectivity. Specifically, let us examine Bolingbroke and Richard as we encounter them in the last act. Representative of familial and customary claims, Bolingbroke is nonetheless seldom shown with his own family. No queen appears by his side, his heir is present in this play only as a nasty rumor, and his other sons will only appear in the second part of *Henry IV*. The family, the classic arena of private life, has been compromised, for Bolingbroke, by his instrumental use of it; he is skillful at deploying other people's families for domination, as in the comic crisis of Aumerle's treason. Lack of familial ties, however, does not exhaust the theme of Bolingbroke's isolation: unlike Richard, who favors the royal "we," Bolingbroke always announces himself as a solitary "I." But like his family relations, Bolingbroke's individuality has lost its subjective force in being used as a political tool. His personality is instrumentalized, as in his equivocal, almost opaque, reaction to Richard's murder: "Though I did wish him dead, / I hate the murtherer, love him murther'd" (5.6.39–40). Throughout the rest of the history cycle, Bolingbroke's most distinctive voice will be heard only in his mourning for his own isolation from his son.

The case of the obsessively subjective Richard is more complex. In his soliloquy at Pomfret Castle, Richard recasts the lament of the deposition scene—"I must nothing be" (4.1.201)—into private terms. Loss of office is for Richard, as it was to be for Othello, loss of public being, but lacking Othello's capacity for desperation, Richard endeavors to create instead an entirely mental world, populated by the creatures of his imagination. That world, to be sure, is compromised by the treason and penury that determine Richard's status as a deposed monarch: his subjectivity cannot substitute social relations for itself. And his invented people fall into the easy categories of public life: they are ambitious or scoundrels, royal or impoverished. Thus his enterprise, to "people this little world," simply repeats the relations of power that he failed to understand in public life. Finally, the whole project founders upon Richard's corporeality, upon the scandal of the royal body wasted by time.

We can see *Richard II,* then, as an investigation of a number of linked, contradictory pairs:

modern state/communal society
private subjectivity/private property
public life/private life

In all of these pairs, relations between parts and wholes, generalities and specific instances, are at issue: we consider various ways of understanding the relations between individuals and social groups. But the text, as I have said, does not present these pairs to us allegorically. The two main characters cut across these axes, so that the character whose political beliefs are most alien to us today, Richard, presents the most fully developed subjectivity, while Bolingbroke, who is more familiar ideologically, seems subjectively distant and opaque. The typical register of the play, then, links its logic and its rhetoric: we are invited to keep alive the dialectical play of its categories by preserving a mobile imagination; the typical register of the play refuses to allow our sympathies to lie down peacefully next to our prejudices.

For Shakespeare's audience, however, somewhat different problems would have emerged. The royal characters of *Richard II* allowed Shakespeare's audience to reappraise their concept of royal rule. Neither king would have been easily assimilable to Renaissance ideology: neither is a tyrant; neither is fully legitimate. Shakespeare's audience would also have met in the play a representation of the modern state, a state they had encountered but had not yet given a name. The pair, Richard and Bolingbroke, present between them all the claims of customary rule and all the necessities of modern sovereignty. For an age so preoccupied with the themes of obedience and rebellion, such a spectacle must have been vertiginous, since the play endorses neither Richard's retreat to privacy nor Bolingbroke's instrumental subjectivity. Thus the play would have suggested questions its audience had not begun to ask in its more narrowly political discourse. It functioned, then, as a representation: an indication of a world other than the one it depicts; a solemn setting forth of what had been presented to the audience in social life but not recognized.

For us, this representation also prompts reflection on the fundamental relations of public and private. Since the nineteenth century, the play has been accessible less as a meditation on usurpation and legitimacy than as an investigation of the ways that Richard's sensibility is at odds with his royal role. We can see the play as a critique of this kind of subjectivity, of Richard's isolated and interiorized self-interrogation. The play invites us to see his self-consciousness as a displaced sovereignty, as the reflex of an exile from power. Indeed, there is no privacy in this play that is not shaped by relations of domination. We can read the garden scene, in which the queen eavesdrops on gardeners and learns of her husband's deposition, as an overt statement of this theme—there, a character who is a "little better thing than earth" (3.4.78) discusses events of state. But further reflection on this scene would require us to consider the paradoxical status of the Renaissance pastoral, which combined a dream of privacy and seclusion with a tradition of political commentary. Such generic considerations would lead us to connect the Renaissance theme of domination with the modern theme of the public and private, a promising line of thought and one we will take up [elsewhere].

To read *Richard II* as representation, then, is to trace out the relations between individuals and groups that the play calls into question, understanding that those questions phrase themselves differently for different historical audiences. A hermeneutic approach to the play's typical register will not resolve the questions that arise in the course of these reflections: it will surely not answer the questions of traditional criticism by assigning the proper ratios of blame to Richard and Bolingbroke, or evaluating Bolingbroke's coalition tactics. Nor would a hermeneutic approach stop, as we have, at the play's typical register; it would also confront the more puzzling, alien, and resistant aspects of the play. But a hermeneutic approach to the play's typical register does illuminate its intersubjective power. We can use this approach both to analyze the differences between the texts we read and those that Shakespeare's audience encountered and also to show the links, translations, and shared horizons of consciousness that bring these texts together. The play, then, speaks to us, but its location in history has been respected.

Richard II and Bolingbroke

Northrop Frye

In *Richard II* Shakespeare had to make a marriage of convenience between the facts of medieval society, so far as they filtered down to him from his sources, and the Tudor mystique of royalty. That mystique regarded government by a central sovereign to be the form of government most in accord with both human nature and the will of God. It is true that no English sovereign except Henry VIII ever had the unlimited power that was very common on the Continent then and for many centuries thereafter. But still the reigning king or queen was the "Lord's anointed," his or her person was sacred, and rebellion against the sovereign was blasphemy and sacrilege as well as treason. The phrase "Lord's anointed" comes ultimately from the Bible. The Hebrew word Messiah, meaning "the anointed one," is applied in the Old Testament to a lawfully consecrated king, including even the rejected King Saul. The Greek equivalent of Messiah is Christ, and Jesus Christ was regarded as the king of the spiritual world, lawful kings in the physical world being his regents. If a lawful king happened to be a vicious tyrant, that was ultimately the fault of his subjects rather than of him, and they were being punished through him for their sins.

So when Richard II, during the abdication scene particularly, draws so many parallels between his trial and the trial of Christ, he is not comparing himself directly to Christ, but saying that the same

---

From *Northrop Frye on Shakespeare,* edited by Robert Sandler. © 1986 by Northrop Frye. Yale University Press, 1986.

situation, of the world rejecting the Lord's anointed, is being enacted once again. Of these echoes from the Passion in the Gospels, perhaps the most striking is that of Pilate's washing of his hands in a futile effort to make himself innocent of the death of Christ. Bolingbroke uses this image when he is making his first act as the next king, in ordering the execution of Bushy and Green; it is repeated in a contrasting context by Richard:

> Not all the water in the rough rude sea
> Can wash the balm off from an anointed king
> (3.2.54–55)

and explicitly linked with Pilate by Richard in the abdication scene. The closing lines of the play are spoken by Bolingbroke, and express his purpose of going on a crusade "To wash this blood off from my guilty hand."

One awkward question might be raised in connection with this doctrine of the sacredness of the royal person. Suppose you're second in line from the throne, and murder the one who's first in line, do you thereby acquire all the sanctity of the next Lord's anointed? Well, in some circumstances you do. Shakespeare's King John becomes king when his nephew, Prince Arthur, is really in line for the succession, and although the prince technically commits suicide by jumping out of a window, John is certainly not innocent of his murder. John thereby becomes by default the lawful king, and when he dies his son Prince Henry becomes his legitimate heir. The strongest man in the country at the time is Falconbridge, bastard son of Richard I, who would have been king if he were legitimate, and could probably seize power quite easily in any case. But he holds back in favour of Prince Henry, and the play comes to a resounding patriotic conclusion to the effect that nothing can happen "If England to itself do rest but true," which in the context means partly keeping the line of succession intact. You may not find this particular issue personally very involving, but the general principle is that all ideologies sooner or later get to be circumvented by cynicism and defended by hysteria, and that principle will meet you everywhere you turn in a world driven crazy by ideologies, like ours.

A lawful king, as Shakespeare presents the situation, can be ruthless and unscrupulous and still remain a king, but if he's weak or incompetent he creates a power vacuum in society, because the order of nature and the will of God both demand a strong central ruler. So a terrible dilemma arises between a weak king de jure and a de facto power that's certain to grow up somewhere else. This is the central theme of *Richard II*. Richard was known to his contemporaries as "Richard the Redeless," i.e., a king who wouldn't take good advice, and Shakespeare shows him ignoring the advice of John of Gaunt and York. His twenty-year reign had a large backlog of mistakes and oppressions that Shakespeare doesn't need to exhibit in detail. In the scene where his uncle John of Gaunt is dying, John concentrates mainly on the worst of Richard's administrative sins: he has sold, for ready cash, the right of collecting taxes to individuals who are not restrained in their rapacity by the central authority. This forms part of what begins as a superbly patriotic speech: Shakespeare's reason for making the old ruffian John of Gaunt a wise and saintly prophet was doubtless that he was the ancestor of the House of Tudor. We also learn that Richard had a very undesirable lot of court favourites, spent far too much money on his own pleasures, and at the time of the play was involved in a war in Ireland that had brought his finances into a crisis. As we'll see [elsewhere], getting into a foreign war is normally by far the best way of distracting a disaffected people, but Ireland roused no one's enthusiasm.

In the Middle Ages the effective power was held by the great baronial houses, which drew their income from their own land and tenants, many of them serfs; they could raise private armies, and in a crisis could barricade themselves into some very strong castles. In such a situation a medieval king had a theoretical supremacy, but not always an actual one, and, as his power base was often narrower than that of a landed noble, he was perpetually hard up for money. So if he were stuck with a sudden crisis, as Richard II is with the Irish war, he would often have to behave like a brigand in his own country and find pretexts for seizing and confiscating estates. What kind of law does a lawful king represent who resorts to illegal means of getting money? Or, who resorts to means that are technically legal, but violate a moral right?

Depends on what the moral right is. If it's abstract justice, protection of the poor, the representation of taxpayers in government, the right of the individual to a fair trial or the like, forget it. Shakespeare's *King John* never mentions Magna Carta, and *Richard II* never mentions the most important event of the reign, the Peasants' Revolt (twenty years earlier, but the social issues were still there). But if you take private property away from a noble house that's powerful enough to fight back, you're in deep trouble. The Duke of York tries to explain to Richard that his own position as king depends on hereditary succession, and that the same principle applies to a nobleman's right to inherit the property of his father. When Richard seizes John of Gaunt's property, he's doing something that will make every noble family in England say "Who next?" So John's son Henry Bolingbroke gets a good deal of support when he defies Richard's edict of banishment and returns to claim his own. We don't know much about what is going on in Bolingbroke's mind at any one time, and that's largely because he doesn't let himself become aware of the full implications of what he's doing. When he says at first that he merely wants his rights, it's possible that he means that. But this is the point at which Richard's spectacular incompetence as an administrator begins to operate. In the demoralized state of the nation a de facto power begins to gather around Bolingbroke, and he simply follows where it leads, neither a puppet of circumstances nor a deliberately unscrupulous usurper.

The rest of the play is the working out of this de jure and de facto dilemma. Some, like the Duke of York, come over to Henry's side and transfer the loyalty owed the Lord's anointed to him. So, when York's son Aumerle conspires in favour of Richard, York accuses his son of the same treason and sacrilege he'd previously accused Bolingbroke of before he changed sides. In the scene where York insists on the king's prosecuting his son for treason and his duchess pleads for pardon, Bolingbroke is at his best, because he realizes the significance of what's happening. He's made the transition from being the de facto king to being the de jure king as well, and after that all he needs to do is get rid of Richard.

There are others, like the Bishop of Carlisle, who take the orthodox Tudor line, and denounce Bolingbroke for what he is doing to the Lord's anointed. As Shakespeare presents the issue, both sides are right. Henry becomes king, and makes a better king, as such things go, than Richard. When his nobles start quarrelling among themselves in a scene that reads almost like a reprise of his own challenge to Mowbray, he puts all the challenges "under gage," postpones all action, and squashes instantly what could become a dangerous brawl. But the way he came to the throne leaves a curse over the House of Lancaster that starts working out after Henry V's death twenty years or so later. Perhaps the only thing that would really resolve the situation is for Henry IV to go on the crusade he keeps talking about, because killing Moslems is so meritorious an act that it wipes out all previous sins, however grievous. John of Gaunt introduces the theme of crusade, as one of the things England was devoted to in its prime: he was doubtless thinking of the contrast between Richard and his namesake, Richard I, who spent so much of his ten-year reign fighting in the Third Crusade. But Henry's plans to go on a crusade are interrupted by revolts against him, and that again is inevitable: one revolt begets another. He carries on as best he can, and the comforting prophecy that he will die in Jerusalem turns out to apply to the name of a room in the palace of Westminster. It is a particularly savage irony, from Bolingbroke's point of view, that his enemy Mowbray, who, unlike him, was banished for life, should have died fighting in a crusade.

It should be clear by now that Shakespeare is not interested in what we would normally think of as history. What is really happening in history is extremely difficult to dramatize. Shakespeare is interested in chronicle, the personal actions and interactions of the people at the top of the social order. And the centre of his interest is in the kind of dramatic performance involved in being a leader in society, more particularly a king. All social relationships are in a sense theatrical ones: as soon as someone we know appears, we throw ourselves into the dramatic situation that our knowledge of him makes appropriate, and act it out accordingly. If we're alone, like Hamlet or like Richard in prison, we soliloquize; that is, we dramatize ourselves to ourselves. And what we all do, the prince makes history, or chronicle, by doing. In his vision of leadership, Shakespeare often comes curiously close to Machiavelli's *The Prince.* Curiously, because it is practically impossible that Shakespeare could have known Machiavelli's writings, and because Shakespeare's social vision is a deeply conservative one, whereas Machiavelli's was realistic enough to make the horrified idealists of his time give him a reputation in England and elsewhere as the voice of the devil himself. He comes in, for example, to emit cynical sentiments as the prologue speaker of Marlowe's *Jew of Malta.* But the theorist and the dramatist converge on two points: the dramatic nature of leadership and the fact that the qualities of the born leader are not moral qualities.

In ancient times stage actors usually wore masks, and the metaphor of the masked actor has given two words to the language. One is "hypocrite," which is Greek in origin and refers to the actor looking through the mask; the other is "person," which is Latin and refers to his speaking through it. Today we also use the word "persona" to mean the social aspect of an individual, the way he encounters other people. To some extent it's a misleading term, because it implies a real somebody underneath the masks, and, as the soliloquy reminds us, there's never anything under a persona except another persona. What there is is a consistency that limits the variety of social relations to a certain repertoire: that is, Hamlet always sounds like Hamlet, and Falstaff like Falstaff, whatever their roles at the moment. But for Shakespeare, as we'll see [elsewhere], the question of identity is connected with social function and behaviour; in other words with the dramatic self, not with some hidden inner essence.

Well, "hypocrite" is a moral term and "person" is not: we accept that everyone has a personality, but it's supposed to be wrong for people to be hypocrites. Hypocrisy has been called the tribute that vice pays to virtue, but to know that you're saying one thing and thinking another requires a self-discipline that's practically a virtue in itself. Certainly it's often an essential virtue for a public figure. Situations change, and the good leader does what the new situation calls for, not what is consistent with what he did before. When Bolingbroke orders the execution of the king's favourites, one of his gravest charges against them is the way that they have separated the king from the queen, but an act or so later he himself is ordering a much more drastic separation of them. A successful leader doesn't get hung up on moral principles: the place for moral principles is in what we'd call now the PR job. The reputation of being virtuous or liberal or gracious is more important for the prince than the reality of these things, or rather, as in staging a play, the illusion is the reality.

Bolingbroke begins and ends the play, and the beginning and ending are in a most symmetrical relationship. At the beginning there is to be a public duel, or trial by battle, between Bolingbroke and Mowbray, over the murder of Thomas of Woodstock. Although Mowbray belongs to the house of Norfolk, not York, here is in embryo the theme of the eight historical plays: two noblemen quarrelling among themselves, with the king driven to stratagems to maintain his ascendancy. Perhaps a shrewder monarch would have left them to fight it out, on the ground that a duel to the death would get rid of at least one dangerous nobleman, but Richard stops the duel and banishes both, Mowbray for life, Bolingbroke for ten years, later reduced to six. The duellists talk so much that we suspect they're both lying, but it's Bolingbroke who drops the key image of civil war, Cain's murder of his brother Abel:

> That he did plot the Duke of Gloucester's death
> . . . .
> Which blood, like sacrificing Abel's, cries
> Even from the tongueless caverns of the earth.
> (1.1.100–105)

At the end of the play, Bolingbroke, now Henry IV, hints that the death of the imprisoned Richard would be most convenient to him, and his follower Exton carries out the murder, and returns expecting a reward for faithful service. He forgot that leaders have to dissociate themselves immediately from such acts, whether they ordered them or not, and the play closes with Exton banished and Henry saying, "With Cain go wander thorough shades of night," echoing Mowbray's line about his banishment: "To dwell in solemn shades of endless night."

The play is thus enclosed by the image of the first human crime, Cain's murder of his brother, the archetype of all civil wars that follow. In the middle comes the scene of the queen and the gardener. The gardener is addressed as "old Adam's likeness," which means that this is not a garden like Eden, where nothing was "unruly" and there were no weeds, but a garden made from the soil that Adam was forced to cultivate after his fall. Another phrase of the queen's, "To make a second fall of cursèd man," is repeated in a very curious context in *Henry V*. Every fall of every consecrated ruler repeats the original fall of man. Since then, history has proceeded in a series of cycles: Shakespeare's audience was thoroughly familiar with the image he uses constantly in his plays, the wheel of fortune, and would see the entire action of this play, from the murder of Woodstock to the murder of Richard, as a single turn of that wheel. Richard's image for this is that of two buckets, one going up and the other down, "The emptier ever dancing in the air," a most sardonic comment on the sort of person who succeeds in the way that Bolingbroke has succeeded. One corollary from this conception of a wheel of fortune is that in history it is only the past that can be idealized or thought of as heroic or peaceful. The *Henry VI* plays look back to the great and victorious Henry V; the play of *Henry V* looks back to the time of Richard as a time when there was no curse of usurpation on the royal house; and in this play we have John of Gaunt idealizing an earlier time, apparently the reign of Edward III, the reign that saw the Black Death and the beginning of the Hundred Years' War with France.

What keeps the wheel turning is the fact that people are conditioned to a certain reflex about it: whenever there's a change in personnel in the state, the assumption is normally that somehow or other an old age is going to be renewed. As the Duchess of York says to Aumerle after the king has pardoned him, "Come, my old son: I pray God make thee new." The joyful expectation on the part of the people that a new king will give a new life to the nation is put by York into its proper context:

> As in a theatre the eyes of men,
> After a well-graced actor leaves the stage,
> Are idly bent on him that enters next.
>
> (5.2.23–25)

The illusion of movement in history corresponds to the processional aspect of a drama, the series of events that holds the interest. We have to listen on a deeper level, picking up such things as the Cain imagery, to realize that the beginning and the end are much the same point.

We feel this circularity of movement from the very beginning, the ordeal by battle that opens the play. Such ordeals, in medieval times, were surrounded by the most detailed ritual and punctilio. The combatants appeared before the king and formally stated their cases; the king would try to reconcile them; he would fail; he would then allow a trial by battle at a time and place duly stated. As the play goes on, the duel modulates to one between Bolingbroke and King Richard, but the same ritual formality continues, except that there is no longer any question of a fair fight. That is one reason why *Richard II* is written, contrary to Shakespeare's usual practice, entirely in verse: no contrasting force from outside the duelling ritual breaks in to interrupt the action.

Bolingbroke realizes that one of the qualities of the leader is inscrutability, giving the impression that there are great reserves of power of decision not being expressed. Of course many people look inscrutable who are merely stupid: Bolingbroke is not stupid, but he understands that the leaders who attract the greatest loyalty and confidence are those who can suggest in their manner that they have no need of it. Later, in *1 Henry IV*, Bolingbroke is telling his son Prince Hal that, in the dramatic show a leader puts on, the one essential is aloofness. He says that he appeared publicly very seldom, and always with calculation:

> By being seldom seen, I could not stir
> But like a comet I was wond'red at
>
> (*1 Henry IV*, 3.2.46–47)

and contrasts his own skilful performance with Prince Hal's wasting time with low company in Eastcheap, which he says is repeating the mistake of "the skipping king" Richard, who lost his crown mainly because he was seen too often and not with the right people. What Henry says may be true as a general political principle, though whether it was true of his own behaviour at the time or not is another question: certainly the communiqué from Richard's headquarters about Bolingbroke is very different from what Bolingbroke remembers of it:

> Off goes his bonnet to an oyster-wench;
> A brace of draymen bid God speed him well
> And had the tribute of his supple knee.
>
> (*Richard II,* 1.4.31–33)

One aspect of this question of leadership has been studied in a fine piece of scholarship, a book called *The King's Two Bodies*, by E. H. Kantorowicz. Oversimplifying a bit, the king's two bodies, as distinguished in medieval and Renaissance theory, are his individual body as a man and his symbolic aspect as the body of his nation in an individual form. To extend this in the direction of *Richard II,* if the individual man is A, and the symbol of the nation as a single body is B, then the real king is B, the consecrated and sacrosanct figure, the king de jure. But the stronger the king is as an individual, and the more de facto ability he has, the more nearly A will equal B, and the better off both the king and his society will be. In any case, whether A equals B or not, it is clear that A minus B equals nothing, and that equation is echoed in the words "all" and "nothing" that run through the abdication scene, and in fact are continuing as late as *King Lear.*

Richard has been brought up to believe in the sanctity of his office, and unfortunately that has not made him more responsible but less so. Hence he turns to magic and fantasy as soon as he is even momentarily frustrated. When he goes to see the dying John of Gaunt, thinking of how soon he can get his money, he soliloquizes:

> Now put it, God, into the physician's mind
> To help him to his grave immediately!
>
> (1.4.59–60)

This is not the voice of a strong-willed and powerful king, but of a spoiled child, and those who talk in such accents can never get away with what they do for long. John of Gaunt tells him his flatterers have got inside his individual castle, and have cut him off from that identification with his society that every genuine king must have. Nobody could express the doctrine of the two bodies more clearly than John of Gaunt does:

> A thousand flatterers sit within thy crown,
> Whose compass is no bigger than thy head;
> And yet, incagèd in so small a verge,
> The waste is no whit lesser than thy land.
> (2.1.100–103)

After his return from Ireland, Richard refuses for a time to believe that anything can affect an anointed king adversely. But after the roll call of disasters has been recited to him he suddenly reverses his perspective, fascinated by the paradox that an individual, as vulnerable and subject to accident as anyone else, could also be the body of his whole kingdom. In short, he turns introvert, and that is a dangerous thing for a ruler to be who expects to go on being a ruler.

It is obvious, long before his final murder, that Richard is no coward, but his growing introversion gives him some of the weaknesses that make other men cowards. One of them is an overreacting imagination that sketches the whole course of a future development before anyone else has had time to figure out the present one. Sometimes these flashes of the future are unconscious: at the beginning he tells Mowbray that he is not favouring Bolingbroke and would not "Were he my brother, nay, my kingdom's heir." That could pass as the straight thematic anticipation that we've met before in Shakespeare. So, more doubtfully, could his complaint about John of Gaunt's "frozen admonition":

> chasing the royal blood
> With fury from his native residence.
> (2.1.118–19)

But when disaster becomes objective he instantly begins to see himself as the central figure of a secular Passion. When Northumberland reports Bolingbroke's wish for Richard to come down and parley with him in the "base court" (the *basse cour* or lower courtyard of Flint Castle), the symbolism of the whole operation flashes at once through his mind:

> Down, down I come, like glist'ring Phaeton
> . . . .
> In the base court? Base court, where kings grow base
> . . . .

> In the base court? Come down? Down, court! Down, king!
> (3.3.178–82)

So active an imagination makes Richard a remarkable poet, but cripples him as a practical man, because his mental schedule is so different from those of people who advance one step at a time, like Bolingbroke. We are reminded here, as so often in Shakespeare, that successful action and successful timing are much the same thing. His being a day late in returning from Ireland has resulted in twelve thousand Welshmen, on a rumour that he was dead, deserting to Bolingbroke. Very little is said about fortune or fate or the stars here, because Richard has made so many mistakes in timing that something like this was bound to hit him sooner or later.

Eventually Richard comes to understand, if not consciously at first, that he is programming himself as a loser, and has thrown himself into the elegiac role of one who has lost his throne before he has actually lost it. This in its turn is a kind of self-indulgent retreat from the confronting situation: "that sweet way I was in to despair," as he calls it. In the abdication scene he makes what could look like a last throw of the dice:

> And if my word be sterling yet in England,
> Let it command a mirror hither straight.
> (4.1.264–65)

It is Bolingbroke who gives the order to bring a looking glass: there is nothing sterling about Richard's word anymore. As far as history is concerned, Richard has had it: nothing remains but to find some device for murdering him. But as far as drama is concerned, Richard is and remains the unforgettable central figure, and Bolingbroke is a supporting actor. How does this come about? How does Richard manage to steal the show from Bolingbroke at the very moment when Bolingbroke is stealing his crown?

The reason goes back to the distinction we made earlier between the two forms of mask: the hypocrite and the person. We all have to be persons, and that involves our being hypocrites at times too: there's no way out of that. But Richard is surrounded with nobles solidly encased in hypocrisy of various kinds: many of them, as we'll discover more fully in the next play, are just gangsters glorified by titles and blank verse, and all of them, including Bolingbroke, are engaged in pretending that a bad king is being deposed for a good one. Some truth in it, of course; there's always a lot of truth in hypocrisy.

When Richard says he sees traitors before him, that is only what a loser would be expected to say. But when he goes on:

> Nay, if I turn mine eyes upon myself,
> I find myself a traitor with the rest
> (4.1.247–48)

he may sound as though he were saying what Northumberland is trying to bully him into saying, or signing: that he is justly deposed as a criminal. But in fact something else is happening: in that solid mass of rebels ritually carrying out a power takeover, Richard is emerging as a stark-naked personality, and the others can do nothing but stare at it.

There follows the inspired mirror scene, in which he dramatizes his phrase "turn mine eyes upon myself." He's still putting on an act, certainly; but it's a totally different act from what he was expected to put on. In one of his two aspects, the king is a human being: by forcing everyone to concentrate on him as a human being, while he stares in the mirror, a kind of royalty becomes visible from that humanity that Bolingbroke will never in this world find the secret of. We see a principle that we see later on in *King Lear:* that in some circumstances the real royalty is in the individual person, not in the symbolic one. Bolingbroke lives in a world of substance and shadow: power is substantial to him, and Richard with his mirror has retreated to a world of shadows. But a nagging doubt remains, of a kind related to the close of *A Midsummer Night's Dream:* which has the more effective power, the Duke of Athens or the king of shadows in the wood? In the context of a history the issue is clearer cut than in a fantastic comedy, of course, except for the audience's response. The audience takes Richard out of the theatre, and groups everyone else around him.

The contrast between what Bolingbroke has become and what Richard has been all along comes out in the two final episodes of the play. The first episode is the one we've glanced at already: Bolingbroke's pardoning of Aumerle, who conspired against him, in response to the impassioned pleas of the Duchess of York. In this episode there are two themes or verbal phrases to be noticed: the theme of the beggar and the king, and the theme of setting the word against the word. Bolingbroke is now king, and everyone else becomes in a sense a beggar: if a subject does anything that puts his life in danger, he must sue to the king for his life as a beggar would do. The "word" being discussed is the word of royal command, specifically the word "pardon." The Duke of York, as hot for prosecuting his son as ever, urges Bolingbroke to say pardon in French, where *pardonnez-moi* would have the general sense of "sorry, nothing doing." But Bolingbroke knows that he is now in a position where he is the source of the word of command, and must make all such words as unambiguous as possible, even when he does what he is soon to do to Exton.

This scene is immediately followed by Richard's great prison speech, which in many respects sums up the play, and repeats these two themes of the beggar and the king and of setting the word against the word. The prison is the final actualizing of the individual world dramatized by the mirror earlier, and Richard is fascinated by the number of personae he can invoke. His soul and brain become an Adam and an Eve, and they germinate between them a whole new world of thoughts. Some of the thoughts are ambitious, wanting only to get out; some are resigned (perhaps Boethius, writing *The Consolation of Philosophy* while awaiting execution in prison, is in the background here), but all of them are discontented. Not because of the prison: they'd be discontented anywhere. Here, setting "the word against the word" refers to the words of Scripture, the commands that come from the spiritual world and so often seem ambiguous; and the king and beggar are the same identity, different only in mask and context. He concludes:

> Nor I, nor any man that but man is,
> With nothing shall be pleased till be he eased
> With being nothing.
>
> (5.5.39–41)

Ever since the beginning of language, probably, "nothing" has meant two things: "not anything" and "something called nothing." Richard is saying here (not very grammatically) that every human being, including himself, is discontented, not pleased with anything, until he becomes that something we call nothing, i.e., in this context, dead. This double meaning becomes very central in *King Lear* later.

In *A Midsummer Night's Dream* the two worlds of the play, Theseus's court and Oberon's wood, represent two aspects of the mind, the conscious, rational, daylight aspect and the dreaming and fantasizing aspect. One dwells in a world of things and the other in a world of shadows; the shadow mind may live partly in the imaginary, in what is simply not there, but it may live partly also in the genuinely creative, bringing into existence a "transfigured" entity, to use Hippolyta's word, which is neither substantial nor shadowy, neither illusory nor real, but both at once. In *Romeo and Juliet* we got one tantalizing glimpse of this world in Mercutio's Queen Mab speech, but what we see of it mostly is the world created out of the love of the two young people, a world inevitably destroyed as the daylight world rolls over it, but possessing a reality that its destruction does not disprove.

Richard II is in a more complex social position, and has been caught in the paradox of the king, who, we remember, possesses both an individual and a sacramental body. The latter includes all the subjects in his kingdom; the former, only himself. In the prison, however, an entire world leaps into life within his own mind: the other world he was looking for in the mirror. He has as many thoughts as he has subjects, and, like his subjects, his thoughts are discontented, rebellious and conflicting. But the king's two bodies are also God's two realities, linked by the anointing of the king.

The imagery changes as music sounds in the background: Richard comments on the need for keeping time in music, and applies the word to his own life: "I wasted time, and time doth now waste me." From there two conceptions of time unfold: time as rhythm and proportion, the inner grace of life itself that we hear in music, and time as the mechanical progress of the clock, the time that Bolingbroke has kept so accurately until the clock brought him to power. Near the beginning of the play, John of Gaunt refuses to take active vengeance for Woodstock's death on the Lord's anointed. He leaves vengeance to heaven, which will release its vengeance "when they see the hours ripe on earth." The word "they" has no antecedent: John must mean something like "the gods," but the image of ripening, and of acting when the time is "ripe," brings in a third dimension of time, one that we don't see in this play, or perhaps fully anywhere else, although there are unconscious commitments to it like Edgar's "ripeness is all." There is a power in time, with its own rhythm and form: if we can't see it in action, perhaps it sees us, and touches the most sensitive people, such as Hamlet, with the feeling that it shapes our ends. If we did see it, perhaps the world of history would burst like an eggshell and a new kind of life would come forth.

Chronology

1564	William Shakespeare born at Stratford-on-Avon to John Shakespeare, a butcher, and Mary Arden. He is baptized on April 26.
1582	Marries Anne Hathaway in November.
1583	Daughter Susanna born, baptized on May 26.
1585	Twins Hamnet and Judith born, baptized on February 2.
1588–90	Sometime during these years, Shakespeare goes to London, without family. First plays performed in London.
1590–92	*The Comedy of Errors,* the three parts of *Henry VI.*
1593–94	Publication of *Venus and Adonis* and *The Rape of Lucrece,* both dedicated to the Earl of Southampton. Shakespeare becomes a sharer in the Lord Chamberlain's company of actors. *The Taming of the Shrew, The Two Gentlemen of Verona, Richard III, Titus Andronicus.*
1595–97	*Romeo and Juliet, Richard II, King John, A Midsummer Night's Dream, Love's Labor's Lost.*
1596	Son Hamnet dies. Grant of arms to Shakespeare's father.
1597	*The Merchant of Venice, Henry IV, Part 1.* Purchases New Place in Stratford.
1598–1600	*Henry IV, Part 2, As You Like It, Much Ado about Nothing, Twelfth Night, The Merry Wives of Windsor, Henry V,* and *Julius Caesar.* Moves his company to the new Globe Theatre.
1601	*Hamlet.* Shakespeare's father dies, buried on September 8.
1601–2	*Troilus and Cressida.*
1603	Death of Queen Elizabeth; James VI of Scotland becomes James I of England; Shakespeare's company becomes the King's Men.
1603–4	*All's Well That Ends Well, Measure for Measure, Othello.*

1605–6	*King Lear, Macbeth.*
1607	Marriage of daughter Susanna on June 5.
1607–8	*Timon of Athens, Antony and Cleopatra, Pericles, Coriolanus.*
1608	Shakespeare's mother dies, buried on September 9.
1609	*Cymbeline,* publication of sonnets. Shakespeare's company purchases Blackfriars Theatre.
1610–11	*The Winter's Tale, The Tempest.* Shakespeare retires to Stratford.
1612–13	*Henry VIII, The Two Noble Kinsmen.*
1616	Marriage of daughter Judith on February 10. Shakespeare dies at Stratford on April 23.
1623	Publication of the Folio edition of Shakespeare's plays.

Contributors

HAROLD BLOOM, Sterling Professor of the Humanities at Yale University, is the author of *The Anxiety of Influence, Poetry and Repression,* and many other volumes of literary criticism. His forthcoming study, *Freud: Transference and Authority,* attempts a full-scale reading of all of Freud's major writings. A MacArthur Prize Fellow, he is general editor of five series of literary criticism published by Chelsea House. During 1987–88, he served as Charles Eliot Norton Professor of Poetry at Harvard University.

RUTH NEVO is Professor of English at Hebrew University in Jerusalem. She is the author of *The Dial of Virtue, Comic Transformations in Shakespeare,* and *Tragic Form in Shakespeare.* She has also translated into English the *Selected Poems* of Chaim Nachman Bialik.

MAYNARD MACK, Jr., is Associate Professor of English at the University of Maryland, College Park. He is the author of *Killing the King.*

STEPHEN BOOTH, Professor of English at the University of California, Berkeley, is the author of *An Essay on Shakespeare's Sonnets* and the editor of *Shakespeare's Sonnets.*

JAMES L. CALDERWOOD is Professor of English and Comparative Literature and Associate Dean of Humanities at the University of California, Irvine. His books on Shakespeare's plays include *Shakespearean Metadrama* and *Metadrama in Shakespeare's Henriad.*

HARRY BERGER, JR., is Professor of English at the University of California at Santa Cruz. He is the author of *The Allegorical Temper* and numerous articles on Spenser and Shakespeare.

SUSAN WELLS is a member of the Department of English at Wayne State University. She is the author of *The Dialectics of Representation*.

NORTHROP FRYE is University Professor Emeritus at the University of Toronto. His major works include *Fearful Symmetry, Anatomy of Criticism,* and *The Great Code: The Bible and Literature*.

Bibliography

Altick, Richard. "Symphonic Imagery in *Richard II.*" *PMLA* 42 (1947): 339–65.

Barkan, Leonard. "The Theatrical Consistency of *Richard II.*" *Shakespeare Quarterly* 29 (1978): 5–19.

Becker, George Joseph. *Shakespeare's Histories.* New York: Ungar, 1977.

Bergeron, David M. *Pageantry in the Shakespearean Theater.* Athens: University of Georgia Press, 1985.

Berry, Edward I. *Patterns of Decay: Shakespeare's Early Histories.* Charlottesville: University of Virginia Press, 1975.

Bethell, S. L. *Shakespeare and the Popular Dramatic Tradition.* Durham, N.C.: Duke University Press, 1944.

Blanpied, John W. *Time and the Artist in Shakespeare's English Histories.* Newark: University of Delaware Press, 1983.

Boris, Edna Zwick. *Shakespeare's English Kings, the People and the Law.* Rutherford, N. J.: Associated University Presses, 1978.

Burckhardt, Sigurd. *Shakespearean Meanings.* Princeton: Princeton University Press, 1968.

Campbell, Lily B. *Shakespeare's Histories: Mirrors of Elizabethan Policy.* San Marino, Calif.: Huntington Library, 1947.

Champion, Larry S. *Perspective in Shakespeare's English Histories.* Athens: University of Georgia Press, 1980.

Cluck, Nancy A. "Shakespearean Studies in Shame." *Shakespeare Quarterly* 36 (1985): 141–51.

Dash, Irene G. *Wooing, Wedding, and Power: Women in Shakespeare's Plays.* New York: Columbia University Press, 1981.

Dean, Leonard F. "*Richard II*: The State and the Image of the Theater." *PMLA* 67 (1952): 211–18.

Driver, Tom F. *The Sense of History in Greek and Shakespearean Drama.* New York: Columbia University Press, 1960.

Dusinberre, Juliet. *Shakespeare and the Nature of Women.* London: Macmillan, 1975.

Faber, M. D. *The Design Within: Psychoanalytic Approaches to Shakespeare.* New York: Science House, 1970.

Fiedler, Leslie. *The Stranger in Shakespeare.* New York: Stein & Day, 1972.

Gaudet, Paul. "The 'Parasitical' Counselors in Shakespeare's *Richard II*: A Problem in Dramatic Interpretation." *Shakespeare Quarterly* 33 (1982): 142–54.

Goddard, Harold C. *The Meaning of Shakespeare.* 2 vols. Chicago: University of Chicago Press, 1951.

Gupta, S. C. Sen. *Shakespeare's Historical Plays.* London: Oxford University Press, 1964.

Hamilton, Donna B. "The State of Law in *Richard II.*" *Shakespeare Quarterly* 34 (1983): 5–17.

Hawkes, Terence. *Shakespeare's Talking Animals: Language and Drama in Society.* Totowa, N.J.: Rowman & Littlefield, 1973.

Holderness, Graham. *Shakespeare's History.* New York: St. Martin's, 1985.

Holland, Norman. *Psychoanalysis and Shakespeare.* New York: McGraw-Hill, 1966.

Humphries, Arthur Raleigh. *Shakespeare:* King Richard II. London: E. Arnold, 1967.

Kahn, Coppélia. *Man's Estate: Masculine Identity in Shakespeare.* Berkeley and Los Angeles: University of California Press, 1981.

Kelly, Henry A. *Divine Providence in the England of Shakespeare's Histories.* Cambridge: Harvard University Press, 1970.

Kernan, Alvin B. "The Henriad: Shakespeare's Major History Plays." In *Modern Shakespearean Criticism: Essays on Style, Dramaturgy, and the Major Plays,* edited by Alvin B. Kernan. New York: Harcourt, Brace & World, 1970.

Knight, G. Wilson. *Shakespeare's Dramatic Challenge.* London: Croom Helm, 1977.

Kott, Jan. *Shakespeare Our Contemporary.* Translated by Boleslaw Taborski. Garden City, N.Y.: Anchor, 1966.

Levy, Fred Jacob. *Tudor Historical Thought.* San Marino, Calif.: Huntington Library, 1967.

Lindenberger, Herbert. *Historical Drama.* Chicago: University of Chicago Press, 1975.

MacDonald, Robert R. "Uneasy Lies: Language and History in Shakespeare's Lancastrian Tetralogy." *Shakespeare Quarterly* 35 (1984): 22–39.

MacKenzie, Clayton G. "Paradise and Paradise Lost in *Richard II.*" *Shakespeare Quarterly* 37 (1986): 318–39.

McMillin, Scott. "Shakespeare's *Richard II*: Eyes of Sorrow, Eyes of Desire." *Shakespeare Quarterly* 35 (1984): 40–52.

Manheim, Michael. *The Weak King Dilemma in the Shakespearean History Play.* Syracuse, N.Y.: Syracuse University Press, 1973.

Newlin, Jeanne T. Richard II: *Critical Essays.* New York: Garland, 1984.

Ornstein, Robert. *A Kingdom for a Stage: The Achievement of Shakespeare's History Plays.* Cambridge: Harvard University Press, 1972.

Palmer, John. *Political Characters of Shakespeare.* London: Macmillan, 1961.

Pierce, Robert B. *Shakespeare's History Plays, the Family and the State.* Columbus: Ohio State University Press, 1971.

Potter, Lois. "The Antic Disposition of Richard II." *Shakespeare Survey* 27 (1974): 33–41.

Prior, Moody. *The Drama of Power: Studies in Shakespeare's History Plays.* Evanston, Ill.: Northwestern University Press, 1973.

Rabkin, Norman. *Shakespeare and the Problem of Meaning.* Chicago: University of Chicago Press, 1981.

Rackin, Phyllis. "The Role of the Audience in Shakespeare's *Richard II.*" *Shakespeare Quarterly* 36 (1985): 262–81.

Ranald, Margaret Loftus. "Women and Political Power in Shakespeare's Histories." *Topic* 36 (1982): 54–65.
Reese, M. M. *The Cease of Majesty: A Study of Shakespeare's History Plays.* London: E. Arnold, 1961.
Ribner, Irving. *The English History Play in the Age of Shakespeare.* London: Methuen, 1965.
Rossiter, A. P. *Angel with Horns and Other Shakespeare Lectures.* Edited by Graham Storey. New York: Theatre Arts Books, 1961.
Saccio, Peter. *Shakespeare's English Kings.* London: Oxford University Press, 1977.
Siegel, Paul N. *Shakespeare's English and Roman History Plays: A Marxist Approach.* Rutherford, N. J.: Fairleigh Dickinson University Press, 1986.
Smidt, Kristian. *Unconformities in Shakespeare's History Plays.* London: Macmillan, 1982.
Spivak, Bernard. *Shakespeare and the Allegory of Evil.* New York: Columbia University Press, 1958.
Sypher, Wylie. *The Ethic of Time: Structures of Experience in Shakespeare.* New York: Seabury, 1976.
Thayer, C. G. *Shakespearean Politics: Government and Misgovernment in the Great Histories.* Athens: Ohio University Press, 1983.
Tillyard, E. M. W. *Shakespeare's History Plays.* London: Chatto & Windus, 1944.
Traversi, Derek. *Shakespeare from* Richard II *to* Henry V. Stanford: Stanford University Press, 1957.
Waith, Eugene M., ed. *Shakespeare: The Histories.* Englewood Cliffs, N. J.: Prentice-Hall, 1965.
Watson, Robert N. "Horsemanship in Shakespeare's Second Tetralogy." *English Literary Renaissance* 13 (1983): 274–300.
Wells, Stanley. "The Lamentable Tale of *Richard II.*" *Shakespeare Studies* 17 (1978–79): 1–23.
Whitaker, Virgil K. *The Mirror up to Nature.* San Marino, Calif.: Huntington Library, 1965.
Wilders, John. *The Lost Garden.* London: Macmillan, 1978.
Wilson, F. P. "The English History Play." In *Shakespearean and Other Studies,* edited by Helen Gardner, 1–53. Oxford: Clarendon, 1969.
Winny, James. *The Player King: A Theme of Shakespeare's Histories.* New York: Barnes & Noble, 1968.

Acknowledgments

"The Genre of *Richard II*" (originally entitled "*Richard II*") by Ruth Nevo from *Tragic Form in Shakespeare* by Ruth Nevo, © 1972 by Princeton University Press. Reprinted by permission of Princeton University Press.

"This Royal Throne Unkinged" by Maynard Mack, Jr., from *Killing the King: Three Studies in Shakespeare's Tragic Structure* by Maynard Mack, Jr., © 1973 by Yale University. Reprinted by permission of Yale Univeristy Press.

"Syntax as Rhetoric in *Richard II*" by Stephen Booth from *Mosiac: A Journal for the Comparative Study of Literature and Ideas* 10, no.3 (Spring 1977), special issue "Shakespeare Today," © 1977 by the University of Manitoba Press. Reprinted by permission of *Mosaic*.

"*Richard II* to *Henry IV*: Variations on the Fall" by James L. Calderwood from *Metadrama in Shakespeare's Henriad* by James L. Calderwood, © 1979 by the Regents of the University of California. Reprinted by permission of the University of California Press.

"Psychoanalyzing the Shakespeare Text: The First Three Scenes of the *Henriad*" by Harry Berger, Jr., from *Shakespeare and the Question of Theory*, edited by Patricia Parker and Geoffrey Hartman, © 1985 by Harry Berger, Jr. Reprinted by permission of Methuen & Co. and the author.

"The Typical Register in Shakespeare's *Richard II*" by Susan Wells from *The Dialectics of Representation* by Susan Wells, © 1985 by The Johns Hopkins University Press, Baltimore/London. Reprinted by permission.

"Richard II and Bolingbroke" (originally entitled "The Bolingbroke Plays [Richard II, Henry IV]") from *Northrop Frye on Shakespeare*, edited by Robert Sandler, © 1986 by Northrop Frye. Reprinted by permission of Fitzhenry & Whiteside and Yale University Press.

Index

PR
2820
.W55
1988

PR
2820
.W55

1988

1/25.94